*Getting There*

# JOB HUNTING FOR WOMEN

## Second Edition

## MARGARET WALLIS

**KOGAN PAGE**

First published in Great Britain in 1987 by
Kogan Page Limited, 120 Pentonville Road,
London N1 9JN. Second edition 1990.

**British Library Cataloguing in Publication Data**
A CIP record for this book is available from the British Library.

ISBN 0-7494-0305-5

Printed and bound in Great Britain by
Biddles Ltd, Guildford

# Contents

# Preface

Why a book for women? Surely men have problems too, in jobhunting and in other aspects of their lives? Of course they do. In my 12 years as a careers adviser I have heard a lot about such problems and I hope that during this time my sympathetic ear and my suggestions have proved helpful to all those who have consulted me. Women often face additional problems, sometimes within themselves, more frequently outside. This book attempts to redress the balance, to show that there are ways of overcoming what are sometimes felt, or assumed, to be inequalities and unfairness. Above all, it aims to encourage women to think about themselves positively.

While revising this book, Tracy Edwards and the crew of *Maiden* returned home triumphantly from the Whitbread Round the World Yacht Race. This feat symbolises the message I wish to convey in the following pages. Be clear what you want and why and how. Don't assume you have to take no for an answer. Trust in your own abilities and judgement. Believe that you can do it. There's every chance that you will.

*Margaret Wallis*
*University of Warwick*
*June 1990*

# Introduction

Final year students frequently expend a lot of time and nervous energy wondering and worrying about what lies ahead. A fortunate few have clear ideas about what they want and how to get it. The majority flounder for varying lengths of time muttering, 'I haven't a clue . . . help!' This book is for them.

Making decisions is difficult for everyone. Making that first career decision is especially difficult. For the 21-year-old student it is often the first big decision in a life so far characterised by success at educational snakes and ladders – good school examination results and on to higher education with scarcely a thought. Certainly subtle – and not so subtle – pressures might have been present. 'All my friends were going on so I didn't want to be different'; 'I couldn't think what else to do – it was a way of postponing a decision'; 'My parents had set their hearts on my going'; 'My teachers all assumed I would' are common explanations.

That is now part of your personal history. Here *you* are facing a novel situation in *your* life. A chance for a change, a new beginning. How can you make a decision? How will you know it is right for you? How might you convince someone else that it is right? How can you make an effective case for yourself to an employer? What factors will influence your choice and who will affect (and be affected by) it? And what if you are not the traditional 21-year-old graduate facing the world of work for the first time? Irrespective of your age and background, what images do the words 'work' and 'career', or the phrases 'working woman' or 'career woman', conjure up in your mind?

Of course, all jobhunters face most of these questions in general terms. Women jobhunters face them and a lot more too. This book is for them, their friends, advisers and employers. Women jobhunting in the 1990s are obviously entering a different world from that of their mothers and grandmothers. They perhaps expect more, and more is expected of them.

This book does not offer a blueprint for action. It does not make your decisions for you. It is not designed as a comfortable read. It offers general advice, but also encourages you to face questions which may be difficult, and alerts you to the wide range of choices that is available. It is not designed as a workbook, several of which are on the market and/or in careers services. The further reading lists will enable you to research more if you wish; they are intentionally a mixture of academic and popular writing.

Above all, this is an optimistic book. It may be true that women face certain problems in jobhunting which their male colleagues avoid simply by being male, but it is also true that today's women jobhunters face a wider choice of jobs and life-styles than ever before. An exciting challenge indeed.

# Acknowledgements

There are no personal dedications. Those who lent their unqualified support to this project know who they are and I thank them unreservedly. Thanks are one thing, responsibility is another: that is mine. In preparing a revised edition of this book I have incorporated several helpful suggestions made by readers of the original version.

I am grateful to the following authors and publishers for permission to quote material as follows:

The Royal Society (1986), *Girls and Mathematics*; Dale Spender (1980), *Learning to Lose*, The Women's Press; College Board, New York (1978), *How to Decide*, Avon; Careers Services Trust of the Association of Graduate Careers Advisory Services (1985), *Issues for Women Students*; Advocacy Press, Santa Barbara, California (1984) for adaptation from *Choices*; National Advisory Body for Public Sector Higher Education (1986), *Transferable Personal Skills in Employment*; Careers Services Trust, Standard Application Form; Eimicke Associates Inc, *Application for Employment*; Ford Motor Company Limited; Marilyn Davidson *et al*, for several sources; Brenda Jones (1982), *Getting Ahead*, Ebury; Natasha Josefowitz (1986), *Paths to Power*, Columbus Books; Judi Marshall (1984), *Women Managers: Travellers in a Male World*, John Wiley & Sons; Virginia Novarra (1980), *Women's Work, Men's Work*, Marion Boyars; Hackney Job Share Project (1982), Institute of Manpower Studies (1985), *Women, Career Breaks and Re-entry*; Margery Povall (1981), *Managing or Removing the Career Break*, Manpower Services Commission; Engineering Council (1985), *Career Breaks for Women Chartered and Technician Engineers*; Jean Martin and Ceridwen Roberts (1984), *Women and Employment*, Her Majesty's Stationery Office; D Perry, *What Else Can a Housewife Do?*, HMSO/MSC/COIC (1983); Natasha Josefowitz (1987), *People Management*, Columbus Books; Equal Opportunities Commission (1989), *The Fact About Women Is . . .*; *Labour Market Quarterly Review* (May 1990), Employment Department; *Social Trends* (1990), Central Statistical Office, HMSO; Anna Alston and Ruth Miller (1989), *Hours to Suit*, Rosters; Anna Alston and Ruth Miller (1987), *Equal Opportunities: A Careers Guide for Women and Men*, Penguin; Rosemary Crompton and Kay Sanderson (1990), *Gendered Jobs and Social Change*, Unwin Hyman; Career Services Trust (1989), *What Do Graduates Do?*, Hobsons Publishing; Committee of Vice Chancellors and Principals (1990), *University Factsheet: Access (Women)*; *Sex Discrimination Act* (1975), HMSO; Equal Opportunities Commission (1983), *So You Think You've Got It Right . . .*; Shelley Adams (1980), *Law at Work: Sex Discrimination*, Sweet and Maxwell.

# Chapter 1
# The Background

Some myths are very pervasive and powerful in our culture. One such myth is the modern equivalent of the knight on a white charger whisking the beautiful maiden away to a life of wedded bliss. Reality for most people is rather different. Yet many of our attitudes to each other and our expectations of behaviour and aspirations are based on assumptions that are as far removed from reality. Assumptions about the typical family, work patterns, educational achievements, the structure of certain professions and numerous other topics are not always supported by facts. Some facts related to women in society are included in Appendix 1; they may surprise you. As you start your jobhunting it is useful to put your own situation in a wider context.

In many cultures it has been argued for generations that there is a relationship between educational attainment and access to certain jobs and therefore salaries. Potent though 'education for education's sake' might be, it is the interlinked relationship between social status and financial gain which has proved most influential. You may have had family arguments about this when selecting your degree course – your first introduction to the world of stereotypes and assumptions perhaps – 'Good grief girl, do choose something sensible like accountancy not sociology'; 'English! The sooner you learn about the real world of computers the better'; 'Of course we want you to be happy, dear, but why psychology/philosophy etc when there are such sensible subjects like business studies to choose from'; 'Yes, well we do know that the country needs more engineers but why do you have to be the odd one out and choose a man's subject?' And so on round the merry-go-round of family and school life, undermining your decision in insidious ways which are all the more powerful because of their caring context. What is caring is not necessarily well informed. Sociology graduates *can* become accountants, English graduates enter the computer industry and a very wide range of graduates are welcome on management training schemes.

Status tends to derive from the paid work undertaken by individuals and that status is often, though not always, derived from salary.

Many research findings have emphasised the link between education and the greater chance of high lifetime earnings. Women graduates might appear to stand on the threshold of a (relatively) rich future. What is the reality? What subjects do they read? Which occupations do they enter? What share of these educational spin-offs might await *you* in the 'top job' areas? If you look at some of the evidence in Appendix 1 you might be depressed. Bear in mind that these figures represent a considerable improvement over previous years and that all the signs are that an increasing proportion of successful applicants for many jobs will be female and that, for example, the expansion of recruitment of women into financial areas, particularly during the 1970s onwards, will see more of them in senior positions in the 1990s.

## Past influences

In looking ahead it will be necessary to look backwards too. When you look back on *your* life, can you recall what and who influenced your view of yourself, your clothes, hobbies, behaviour, school subjects, what to study in higher education, what you feel you are good at? Early influences are very important. They can include the people you met and what they led you to expect from yourself as well as others. Such 'role models' can include women in various work areas. Thus, you are more likely to believe that women can be doctors or mathematicians if your mother was a doctor and you had an inspired maths teacher at school. Look at the figures in Appendix 1 to see the disparity between the sexes in school examinations, for instance. Mathematics is probably the subject over which most concern is expressed because the possession of basic numerical skills is the key to a wide range of occupations. In a study by the Royal Society (*Girls and Mathematics*, 1986) it was stated that:

> There is no convincing evidence that girls have an innate or genetic disability at mathematics adequate to account for the observed differences in achievement. Many girls do, however, have unfavourable attitudes towards mathematics. The reasons for this are many and varied – sociological, psychological and cognitive factors are all involved. The 'masculinity' of mathematics conflicts with girls' sense of their own femininity, which has been determined from birth by the attitudes and influences of the people and things around them. Teaching styles, methods of interaction, the examination syllabus and modes of assessment also combine subtly to disadvantage girls. It is, of course, acknowledged that there are many individual exceptions where girls like and do well at mathematics.

There are other ways of looking at this question. The following poem neatly summarises the trap:

*Gender and Marketable Skills:*
*Who underachieves at maths and science?*

History tells me
That it is not so long since *languages*
Were considered very important.
Anyone who wanted to get on in the world
Needed languages as an entry qualification
For this was how you sorted those who were capable
From those who were not.

Girls, it seems,
Were not.
They were 'naturally'
Not very good at languages
When languages were required
For leaders.

Today
It is maths and the sciences
Which are considered very important
For those who want to get on in a technological world.
Maths and sciences are the entry qualifications
Which sort those who are capable
From those who are not.

Girls, it seems
Are not.
They are 'naturally'
Not very good at maths and science
While these are required
Of leaders.

Of course,
I could resign myself to accept
That girls are inferior
If it were not for one inconsistency.
Today when languages are not needed,
When they are not used to sort those who are capable
From those who are not,
*Girls have come to be 'naturally' good at languages.*

Have they progressed so far
In such a short time,
I ask myself?
Are they but one century
Behind?
In the twenty-first century,
Will they become
Very good at maths and science?

Possibly.
As long as maths and science
Are not required
As entry qualifications!
It is not that girls have changed so much
In the last 100 years,
It is that the entry qualifications
Have changed.

Tomorrow,
If weaving and cake making
Are considered very important
And those who want to get on in the world
Need them as an entry qualification
Because they sort those who are capable
From those who are not.
Girls, it seems
Will not.
They will be 'naturally'
Not very good at weaving and cake making
When they are required
For leaders.

It's a very convenient arrangement.
It's very clever of those who control the entry qualifications
To be able to control nature as well.
For we can chase our own tails
And spend years
Testing girls for their inadequacies
We will not find them,
For we are looking in the wrong place.
The underachievement lies not in the girls,
But in those who do not wish to accept them,
As equals.

                                                          Dale Spender

That argument has been taken up by researchers at the University of East Anglia whose analysis of qualifications obtained by women led them to conclude that in an increasingly difficult employment situation more people have striven for academic qualifications. This, in turn, has meant that employers have increased their entry requirements, and the nature of some jobs, but not necessarily their titles, has consequently changed. Concern has also been expressed that the effects of the 1981 government cutbacks in expenditure on universities, and reduced/erratic funding elsewhere in the education system, plus the government's declared preference for science and technology courses in particular, will all affect women's chances of higher education unless there is a continuation of the campaign to encourage more girls to study these subjects in school.

In fact there has been a steady increase in the proportion of girls taking school examinations successfully in the full range of subjects, a pattern which is repeated in higher education. The disproportion in some subjects continued to cause concern throughout the 1980s. 1984 was Women into Science and Engineering (WISE) year and the series of events, publications and campaigns which were undertaken showed that numerous able and well-meaning people in industry, commerce, education and government were at their wits' end about how to attract more girls and women into these areas. This was less a belief in equality of opportunity than concern over the nation's future, but the result has been a change in attitudes about the 'sex' of subjects. There have also been some attempts to catch able people later on. The computer industry has been extremely successful in recruiting and training people from a wide range of academic disciplines – graduates of philosophy, music, classics, sociology etc work alongside mathematicians and computer scientists. Since the summer of 1986, the BBC has recruited 'any discipline' graduates to its engineering training scheme. More recently, the Women into Information Technology group has been founded. If the will is there, far more things are possible than has previously been thought. Whatever subjects you studied at school, are studying or hope to study in higher education or through adult education programmes, more doors are open than you might imagine. Dale Spender's poetic analysis may prove to be too depressing given a resurgence of interest in languages for all in view of the Single European Market.

If you are a student or graduate, by getting that far in the education system you are already defined as a success. It is assumed that you will set off on a career. Graduates are not expected to have a 'fill in' mentality epitomised in comments such as, 'Well, it'll do till I marry and have kids.' However, the fact that such attitudes exist, the assumption that somehow domesticity will end problems rather than perhaps start them – all encouraged by romantic fiction and many advertisements – can be an added pressure for women. Men have not traditionally faced such pressure and have appeared to be more in control of their own destiny than women. Throughout the centuries they have been expected to be single-minded in terms of earning a living, finding a mate, defending a territory. Of course, not all men have been able to meet such expectations but few have 'retreated' to a domestic role.

This lack of control, real or imagined, causes various dilemmas for women. Some researchers suggest that women are not independent agents, observing that while most men make plans, most women make 'contingency plans'. Such plans might include job, leisure, children, household activities, community involvement, but men they have not yet met often shadow and distort their thoughts. What kind of career adapts to such contingencies?

Does that strike a chord with you? Are your thoughts confused by such 'what ifs' and perhaps some 'if onlys' too? Some of the implications are discussed in Domestic Issues, page 93. Of course, you may not want a monogamous life-style anyway, or you may prefer single-sex relationships, or have decided already that your personal life is secondary to your career. But circumstances and attitudes can change. Thus, for example, even if you yearn for the statistically unusual nuclear family (Mum, Dad and 2+ children) of the advertisers' target group, illness, separation, divorce and death may affect your dreams and having a career may become a necessity. However uncomfortable such thoughts may be, do look ahead, make plans and contingency plans. And think what *you* want first rather than what you think, or know, others want for you. This book is designed to help you with such thinking and planning.

## Further reading

Acker, S, ed (1984), *Women and Education: World Yearbook of Education*, London, Kogan Page (includes a comprehensive bibliography).

Angrist, S S (1969), 'The Study of Sex Roles', *Journal of Social Issues*, 25, 215–32.

Crompton, R and Sanderson, K (1986), 'Credentials and Careers: Some Implications of the Increase in Professional Qualifications Amongst Women', *Sociology*, Vol 20, No 1.

Crompton, R and Sanderson, K (1990), *Gendered Jobs and Social Change*, London, Unwin Hyman.

Further Education Unit (1981), *Balancing the Equation*, London, HMSO.

Mathematical Education Committee (1986), *Girls and Mathematics*, London, Royal Society.

O'Connor, H *et al.* (1984), *Women in Engineering*, London, Engineering Industry Training Board.

Open University (1983), *The Changing Experience of Women*, Milton Keynes, Open University Press (material for Course U221).

Smail, B (1985), *Girl-Friendly Science: Avoiding Sex Bias in the Classroom*, London, Longman Resource Unit.

Spender, D and Sarah, E, eds (1980), *Learning to Lose: Sexism and Education*, London, Women's Press.

# Chapter 2
# Making Decisions

## Introduction

Phrases such as 'career planning', 'self-knowledge', 'jobhunting skills' are common in careers literature. There is an American book called *If you don't know where you're going you'll probably end up somewhere else*: maybe trite but certainly true. There is ample evidence that those who start their career-thinking early are most likely to achieve their objectives.

*Your* decision about *your* career and future may well be the first real decision you have had to make. Here you are, nearing the end of your higher education experience, teetering on the brink of. . . what? Of course, you are knowledgeable about your academic subject. You have had many life experiences, but serious decision-making may not have been among them. A success of the education system by the very fact of your being in higher education at all, each step following logically from the last, GCSEs/O levels on to A levels, and with good enough grades, you found yourself taking a degree course before you knew where you were. Certainly that pattern is common among undergraduates. It therefore follows that many people around you share your predicament, and many understand the difficulties of the transition to the next stage. Older graduates can face extra difficulties (see Chaper 7).

We all think we know what a decision is: it is what happens when we make up our minds. How simple that sounds. No mention of the sleepless nights, the day-time agonies, the consultations, the research, the if-ing and but-ing that went on beforehand. A decision follows when alternatives have been evaluated. It usually involves an objective, and methods of achieving it. Thus, we weigh up the pros and cons, think of the implications, consider priorities and maybe tactics too, in order to get where we want to be. Such text-book scenarios are much more difficult and confused in practice. To be fair, some books do recognise the problems:

> A decision is an act, and in taking or choosing a specific action, an individual is required to make a commitment of personal resources that cannot be replaced. The resources committed might involve time, money, a personal relationship, a career, a style of life, or even a

19

strongly held belief. A decision might be painful, pleasant, or anxiety-producing, or it might relieve a troubling situation. A decision can be and do all these things, but most of all it means taking action. It means getting off the fence. It can be a way to move you toward what you want or what is important to you and give you freedom and control over your life.

*(How to Decide*, 1978)

Accepting that is frightening, whatever stage in life you have reached. Few of us like to take risks, yet taking decisions means taking risks. The stress involved in making decisions about a career is recognised by many researchers. They refer to the time taken from study in order to jobhunt, the assumption that the first career decision cannot be reversed, and self-disapproval or fear of the disapproval of others, plus various avoidance strategies, all of which compound stress.

Careers advisers, academic staff, friends and relations of students are quite used to hearing, 'I haven't a clue' in answer to well-meaning questions about what lies beyond degree day. Transitions from one role to another are often daunting. One reason for this is that in our culture we tend to 'label' ourselves. For example, you are more likely to describe yourself as a student than as a kind person. This labelling, or defining people according to the paid work that they do, has many linguistic and psychological implications ('I'm only a housewife' and other apologist statements), some of which are particularly noticeable and depressing during a period of high unemployment.

All this places an extra burden on current jobhunters, especially women. Anyone who reads the papers, watches TV news, or talks to those in or out of work, is understandably apprehensive. Certainly, there is a temptation to run away. You can certainly avoid rejection letters and the unpleasant feelings they engender if you don't apply for anything. You can assume that 'There are no jobs so what's the point of applying?' You can assume that, without any further effort on your part, 'Something will turn up, it always has done up to now.' Or you can stave off questions by declaring, 'Oh, I'm taking a year off ' (but then not making any plans for such a period). These and many more tricks are used by students – and others too, of course – to avoid having to make a decision. Ostriches do not make effective jobhunters.

## Looking at yourself

If you want to take responsibility for your own decisions, both now and in the future, you might find it helpful to spend some time formulating your own answers to the following set of questions which appeared in 'Issues for Women Students' (1985), an Association of Graduate Careers Advisory Services Sex Equality Working Party publication. (This is now the Sex Equality Sub-Committee and a new version of 'Issues' is expected during 1990.) These questions might make you feel uncomfortable but they will help you to know yourself better as a person and as a woman, and will prepare you for the next stage, applications and interviews.

- How do we see ourselves? What images do we project to others, and what are the advantages and disadvantages of these images to us?

- Who has influenced our choices in the past? To which person(s) can we attribute our most important assumptions? Have we examined all these assumptions to see if they still have – or have ever had – real relevance for us?

- How have sex-role stereotypes affected attitudes to ourselves and others? Do we tend to retreat behind such stereotypes in difficult circumstances? Does it matter if we do? Do we ourselves create generalised images of women, eg the ambitious, forceful career woman or the quiet, passive woman? If so, what does this tell us about ourselves?

- How is our self-esteem? Is it easily dashed by competition or allegations of non-femininity, for instance? How can confidence be increased? How can we be more assertive, more positive about ourselves without being aggressive? Can we 'hold our own' in seminars, in a discussion, in an interview?

- Do we tend to restrict our sights to traditional 'women's jobs'? Are we realistically flexible in our career aims or are we over-willing to compromise our career aims, to lower our sights?

Most people marry and have children. This fact *undeniably* has a greater effect on the careers of women than those of men, if only because most

- prospective employers anticipate that a female candidate's working life will be affected by marriage. When making career plans, it can be helpful to think through what effects marriage and motherhood may have, how life could be organised.

The following points could be considered:

- Is there a choice between doing paid work and staying at home? What are the implications of having children? Is this a consideration in our career thinking?

- What is our opinion of women who combine motherhood and a full-time career? Conversely, how do we feel about women who make motherhood a full-time occupation?

- What contribution do we expect men to make to childrearing, domestic responsibilities, 'bread-winning'? How could two people jointly go about planning their careers?

- Is applying only to the limited range of employers offering flexible working arrangements (career break schemes, job sharing etc) the answer? Or what about gaining a good range of skills and then using our expertise as a lever to change things from within?

- What about using career breaks constructively: for retraining or keeping up with developments?

This book provides some of the background information which can help you to find answers to such questions. Obviously your answers may differ from the next person's. This book is not advocating rights and wrongs in terms of answers that are sweeping generalisations and very misleading. It *is* saying that there are right and wrong answers for *individuals*, and it aims to help *you* discover what might turn out to be right for *you*. The following example of a common issue in jobhunting illustrates this point.

*Question*: Are there any restrictions on your mobility?
*Comment*: It would be asking for trouble if you are currently involved in a personal relationship which feels as if it will be long term, if you have already discovered that neither of you can bear to be apart for more than a few hours (and even that with difficulty), and you then apply for a job in which there are regular moves around the country over which you have no control, and your partner has opted for one of the professions and will spend at least the foreseeable future in one location. Realising that there is a mismatch between your personal life and the requirements of a particular job is helpful because you can then think about possible compromises. Conversely, it would be foolish to assume that all personal relationships are identical and that just because you know you cannot cope with

separation does not mean that the couple next door might not have contrary views and priorities.

If you are an older jobhunter you may wish you had made rather different decisions in the past. Despite the benefit of hindsight, try not to let such thoughts divert you from your current goal – making a good decision *now*.

## Decision-making patterns

'Changed your mind? Women's prerogative.' Phrases of this type are symptomatic of an attitude which gives permission, even respectability, to behaviour patterns which can cause severe problems for individual women and those closest to them. Women who want genuine equality of opportunity should also be prepared to hold equal responsibility, and this includes taking responsibility for their own decisions. That might sound logical but there are difficulties.

As you saw on page 17 there is a tendency for women to define themselves and their aspirations in terms of someone else. Even if you do not do this yourself you will find that other people sometimes define you in this way. A research study at the University of Manchester Institute of Science and Technology noted the vagueness with which many women approached career decision-making and career planning which highlights the ambivalence many women feel when taking actions which give them more control over their own lives, as if this is 'unfeminine', 'too calculating', 'too ambitious'. 'Cupid's dart', 'fate' and 'romance' have little place in such a view of the future and this can be frightening to some.

Decisions can be more difficult for women to make because of the complex mixture of assumptions, prejudices and stereotypes which colour so many attitudes. Thus, worrying about what other people think and being afraid of seeming different can cloud issues and lead to oblique decision-making patterns which might turn out to be wrong for you.

Some examples of such patterns are:

| *Safe* | Definition: | Choosing the alternative that is most likely to bring success. |
| | Example: | Choosing to stay with a familiar subject you know and are good at. |
| *Escape* | Definition: | Choosing an alternative to avoid the worst possible result. |

|  | Example: | Not applying for a job you want because you are afraid you'll be rejected. |
|---|---|---|
| *Compliant* | Definition: | Letting someone else decide, or giving in to group pressure. |
|  | Example: | Applying for chartered accountancy because everyone on your course seems to be doing so. |
| *Intuitive* | Definition: | Making a choice on the basis of vague feelings. |
|  | Example: | Saying 'something in the media would be rather nice' without actually doing anything specific to achieve that goal. |
| *Agonising* | Definition: | Getting so overwhelmed by alternatives that you confuse yourself. |
|  | Example: | Collecting every brochure, directory and broadsheet you can and reading them from cover to cover without any idea of what you're looking for ('I'll know it when I see it'). |
| *Delaying* | Definition: | Procrastination. |
|  | Example: | Delaying going near your careers service until the last afternoon of your last term. |

(Adapted from *Choices*)

You can doubtless think of other behaviour patterns. None of them is very effective when making career decisions.

A rather more effective pattern is one which combines information-gathering with planning. You can state your problem, consider the alternative solutions and the pros and cons of each, and think about the implications.

In order to make an informed decision about a career, as indeed about other matters, you need to work out what you need to know, gather information about it, including a consideration of the alternatives, then consider the possible outcome of the decision.

Jobhunters need to know who is doing the hunting, and what the hunter is looking for.

For example: You are approaching the final year of your course. You want to use your numerical, analytical and literary skills in a professional capacity, preferably in a financial setting. You are ambitious and don't mind working hard. You know there are other financial jobs besides accountancy, but you do not know where these are, what employers' attitudes to women might be, or how/when they recruit. A lot of this information would be provided by your careers service. You might then work out a strategy for applications to certain employers, and possibly also a contingency plan to cover you in case of initial rejection.

You may find that your careers service has one or other of the computerised decision-making aids such as PROSPECT, GRAD-SCOPE, CASCAID-HE, CAOS, JIIG-CAL* or Career Builder which can help you to approach your decision-making in a structured way. Careers services contain vast amounts of information files about different occupations and employers, take-away literature, videos produced by particular employers or professions, in addition to all the help available from experienced advisers.

## Further reading

Bingham, M *et al.* (1984), *Choices*, Watford, Exley.

Janis, I and Mann, L (1977), *Decision-making: A Psychological Analysis of Conflict, Choice and Commitment*, New York, Free Press.

Herriot, P (1984) *Down From the Ivory Tower: Graduates and Their Jobs*, Chichester, John Wiley.

Hopson, B and Scally, M (1984), *Build Your Own Rainbow: A Workbook for Career and Life Management*, Leeds, Lifeskills Associates.

Scholz, N T *et al.* (1978), *How to Decide: A Workbook for Women*, New York, Avon Books.

Skinner, J and Fritchie, R (1988) *Working Choices: A Life Planning Guide for Women Today*, London, J M Dent.

Career education materials available from careers advisory services including the AGCAS *Exploring Your Future* Workbook Series and the video *Starting Points*.

---

* CASCAID-HE=Careers Advisory Service Computer Aid in Higher Education
 CAOS=Computer Aided Option Selector
 JIIG-CAL=Job Ideas and Information Generator-Computer Assisted Learning

## Assertiveness and you

No 1990s book about the world of work would be complete without a reference to assertiveness. There are several books which outline the theory and application of assertiveness so this section will be brief.

Assertiveness is an approach, first to yourself then to other people. It means standing up for your own rights and expressing thoughts, feelings, beliefs and wishes in direct, honest and appropriate ways which do not violate the rights of others. Assertiveness involves respect, first for yourself and then for others rather than deferring to them and their needs or wishes (real or assumed) or putting them down. It can minimise self-criticism, something which is particularly important for women. Assertiveness is *not* aggressiveness or passiveness. There are numerous applications. Here is one example.

| | |
|---|---|
| The scenario: | A friend tries to persuade you to go with her to see a film you've both talked about. You have promised yourself you'd spend the evening drafting your first application form. You could react in the following ways: |
| *Aggressive* | How could you be so inconsiderate? I want to get a job even if you don't. |
| | *or* |
| *Passive* | Oh, all right. What the hell. The form can wait. |
| | *or* |
| *Assertive* | Look, I know we've discussed this film but I didn't know it was on tonight and I've been planning all day how to make a start on these forms. This is important to me. Why don't you try someone else for tonight, or how about trying to get tickets for the Thursday late showing? |

'Assertiveness training' is now a standard component in most training courses. More attention has been given to it in relation to women but it is an approach which is relevant to men too.

### Further reading

Alberti, R E and Emmons, M L (1970), *Your Perfect Right*, San Luis Obispo, California, Impact.

Butler, P E (1976), *Self-Assertion for Women*, San Francisco, Harper & Row.

*Dickson, A (1982), *A Woman in Your Own Right*, London, Quartet Books.

Fisher, R and Ury, W (1989), *Getting to Yes*, London, Hutchinson.

*Horne, K (1990), *The NUS Women's Training Manual*, London, National Union of Students.

Lange, A and Jakubowski, P (1976) *Responsible Assertive Behaviour*, Champaign, Illinois, Research Press.

Phelps, S and Austin, N (1975), *The Assertive Woman*, San Luis Obispo, California, Impact.

*Stewart, J (1989), *Well, No One's Ever Complained Before. . .*, Shaftesbury, Element Books.
*
Stubbs, D R (1985), *Assertiveness at Work*, London, Pan.

*British. The majority of books on this subject are American; most adapt Alberti and Emmons, each with slightly different emphases.

*Chapter 3*
# The Jobhunting Campaign

## The language of jobhunting

Jobhunting has its own jargon. Long before that first interview you will need to familiarise yourself with this jargon. *Career education, decision-making skills, transferable skills, job function* (ie *personnel, marketing, purchasing, production, management services, finance* etc), and many more. You will need to understand the meaning of these words and, as if that wasn't daunting enough, the way in which they are used by different organisations.

Careers advisory services contain a vast array of material which is designed to help you: information booklets, fact sheets, job studies, reference files, details about employers and their past and present vacancies, and much more too. They also host an annual event known as the 'milk round', so called because, just as the milk float calls at various establishments, regular recruiters of graduates undertake a tour of the country – Bristol Polytechnic today, Bath University tomorrow, Reading the day after, and so on – throughout the spring term to give first interviews.

If you are no longer a student and are relying on other sources of information you will still need to familiarise yourself with jargon, perhaps using some of the books listed on page 72. It is also worth sending off for further particulars of jobs advertised in your chosen field as these will often include job descriptions which start to provide a picture of what lies behind some of those words.

No matter what your age, work experience or educational background, there is no substitute for talking to someone who is doing the sort of job you think you might like. This is relatively easy to arrange through previous graduate contact lists, local employer contacts, personal contacts, or even the Yellow Pages. Most people are willing to give up half an hour of their time in this way as it is, of course, flattering to be invited to discuss a subject on which they are the unquestioned expert, namely themselves! Such a tactic has the advantage of making you look sensible in finding out what you might be letting yourself in for, it can convey the 'flavour' of a job, you can obtain anecdotal information about how someone else go in, you can see a work environment and consider whether you can imagine yourself liking it. Reading case studies can be helpful too (see Chapter 8).

## Sexism in language

If you have already started looking through careers literature you may have noticed that some of it seems to assume that most, if not all, jobhunters are male (and white). Thanks to vigorous campaigning by the Equal Opportunities Commission, the Commission for Racial Equality, the Association of Graduate Careers Advisory Services and other groups, there have been some improvements in recent years. Now a great proportion of the language is non-sexist and there is sometimes a spread of photographs, illustrations etc to reflect a multicultural society. How do you react when you read or see images which appear to exclude you? What conclusions do you draw? What examples can you produce from your experience so far?

There is a tendency to use the male pronoun: 'after *he* has done that a good manager will. . .'; 'a candidate should submit *his* claim to. . .'; 'after a few months the trainee can expect that *his* efforts will be rewarded. . .'. There is the condescending, sometimes flirtatious, remark of the type, 'Good morning, gentlemen . . . oops, we mustn't forget the charming Miss Bloggs, must we?' There are a host of well-worn phrases in which men and women frequently collude in a discriminatory use of language. 'She tackled that just like a man.' 'She's just like one of the lads, actually.' 'She can stick to her guns as well as any man.'

Being 'written out' or 'talked down to' may not bother you personally but it is a topic you should be aware of before you start jobhunting because language is one way in which you can pick up clues about the prevailing style and ethos of an employer, and a way in which you can convey something to an employer.

There is now a large amount of literature about language which shows just how pervasive language discrimination can be. Some writers have argued that women have in effect been cut out of many situations – often, sadly, by well-intentioned professionals, notably teachers – and therefore denied opportunities. 'Writing out' of women has also hidden a sense of women as writers, artists, business people and so forth over the centuries. Being aware of this is an important piece of general knowledge (as is knowing about the linguistic origins of the word 'he' and its all-embracing meaning). Being sensitive to the issue of language is important, not only personally but professionally, especially if you are thinking about job specialisms such as personnel or advertising.

Some authors have tried to counterbalance the male, and

unwelcoming, orientation of much writing by using the female pronoun throughout or in alternate chapters. Male readers tend to
notice this first and complain. Many female readers are so
anaesthetised that they do not always spot the difference.

What is *your* attitude to this? Is it sufficiently encouraging to you
to see in minuscule print in a recruitment brochure, or in an advertisement, 'For convenience the male pronoun is used throughout.
Applications from women are of course considered'? Not too many
linguistic gymnastics are required to avoid both female *and* male
pronouns. Doubtless you have already discovered that the attitudes
to sexist language (and other behaviours) vary among your friends
and acquaintances. During jobhunting *you* will have to decide its
significance. Do you think it is a lot of fuss about nothing, or do you
think it matters? There is a wider significance here than those old
jokes about 'personhole covers' and the debate about the pronunci-
ation of 'Ms'. Attitudes lurk behind language and an awareness of
them is certainly relevant to your jobhunting.

## Further reading

Adams, S (1980), *Law at Work*: *Sex Discrimination*, London, Sweet and
Maxwell.

Equal Opportunities Commission (1980), *A Guide to the Equal Treatment
of the Sexes in Careers Materials*, Manchester, EOC.

Equal Opportunities Commission (1980), *The Sex Discrimination Act and
Advertising*, Manchester, EOC.

Equal Opportunities Commission (1983), *So You Think You've Got It
Right. . .* , Manchester, EOC.

Equal Opportunities Commission (1986), *Fair and Efficient – Guidance
on Equal Opportunities Policies in Recruitment and Selection Procedures*,
Manchester, EOC.

Gregory, C (1987), *Sex, Race and the Law*: *Legislating for Equality*, London,
Sage.

Home Office (1978), *Sex Discrimination*: *A Guide to the Sex Discrimination
Act of 1975*, London, HMSO.

Miller, C and Swift, K (1981), *The Handbook of Non-Sexist Writing*, London, Women's Press.

Spender, D (1982), *Man Made Language*, London, Routledge & Kegan
Paul.

Straw, J (1989), *Equal Opportunities*: *The Way Ahead*, London, Institute of
Personnel Management.

**Planning your campaign**

This plan is suitable for a final year student jobhunter. If your circumstances are different, some of the general principles remain valid. Consult the further reading list at the end of Chapter 5.

1. *Decide what you want.*
   - Concentrate on getting a good degree
   - Aim for an academic or vocational postgraduate course
   - Jobhunt (before, or after graduation?)
   - or what?

2. *Decide the job function*
   - Computing, sales, distribution, purchasing etc?

3. *Use your careers advisory service.*
   - Discuss your ideas with a careers adviser
   - Join in: group discussions
     employer presentations and open days
     vacation information courses
     careers information fairs
     Insight into Management courses
     and lots more too.
   - Check the recruitment schedule for the current year, off-site recruiters as well as those visiting, and watch for early deadlines, eg for advertising agencies, market research, some City institutions.

4. *Plan your attack.*
   - Read employer literature. (NB Regular recruiters will send supplies to your careers service who will also hold a set of employer reference files in addition to general occupational information.)
   - If your top choice job area requires an individual approach, learn which advertisement sources are used and keep an eye on those (eg the *Guardian* has 'theme' days for its advertisements, Monday for media, Tuesday for education etc).
   - Familiarise yourself with recruitment trends and practices, eg the sequence of resignation dates and advertisements for teachers, the link between early application for professional social work training and obtaining a funded place.

- Read Finding Out about Vacancies, below.

- Decide on your referees and brief them about your plans.

5. *Be systematic.*
Keep a file containing:

- copies of all correspondence with employers

- job descriptions

- recruitment brochures

- copies of press advertisements followed up

- your current CV (see pages 53–4)

- copies of all application forms sent off, or if you are using the Standard Application Form, (see pages 43–8), keep that plus copies of your answers to some of the essay questions used on other forms

- a time chart recording
    —date you sent off forms
    —date of acknowledgement letter if any
    —date of interview(s)
    —when you heard result
    —any problems or particular points relevant to
       particular applications.

6. *Dare to face up to some of the issues raised elsewhere in this book.*

7. *Determine to be positive about yourself, and to persevere.*


## Finding out about vacancies

Depending on your circumstances some or all of the following will help you to identify vacancies.

### Careers advisory services

Careers services are notified directly of many jobs by letters from individual organisations and through 'Forward Vacancies' and 'Current Vacancies' which are essential sources of information about jobs for graduates. If you have already graduated you can go on a mailing list through your former institution or obtain the vacancy information direct from the Central Services Unit. Employers who participate in the annual 'milk round', conducting first interviews in educational establishments, send additional information, brochures and application forms direct to careers services. Watch out for Summer Recruitment Fairs and Graduate Job Fairs too.

## Graduate directories

*ROGET* (Register of Graduate Employment and Training) is the official guide produced on behalf of the Association of Graduate Careers Advisory Services; it has a parallel computer system, *ROGETSCAN*.

*GET* (Graduate Employment and Training) and *GO* (Graduate Opportunities) plus *DOG* (Directory of Opportunities for Graduates) guides are produced commercially. None of these directories is a vacancy list as such but they do contain entries from many regular recruiters of graduates, providing names and addresses, a brief description of the organisation, and an indication of the type of job specialisms for which vacancies are occasionally available.

## Advertisements

Many organisations place advertisements in the national press and specialist journals. Others concentrate on the latter. Some co-ordinating bodies provide their own advertisements for specialist vacancy bulletins, eg the Arts Council and the Hospital Physicists Association. Sometimes press advertisements are a general encouragement for a range of people to apply, eg for a career in the Armed Services, or the Civil Service. Often they are for a specific vacancy caused by resignation, promotion or expansion.

## Government agencies

During 1990 the employment and training programmes which were previously offered through the Training Agency will become the responsibility of a national network of 80 Training and Enterprise Councils (TECs). At the time of writing these programmes are expected to include Youth Training, Employment Training, Enterprise Allowance Scheme, Small Firms Counselling and Business Growth Training. These programmes will include provision for unemployed graduates and a range of skills-updating activities. Details are available from local Training Agency offices and JobCentres. The Equal Opportunities Commission has suggested that TECs could help to establish local equal opportunities and women's training advisory groups where these do not already exist, to advise on the particular training needs of women.

## Private agencies/Consultancies

There are numerous agencies of variable reputation. They can be worth using if you have some previous work experience. There are some specialist agencies for career changers, for executive development, for women. Some, especially those dealing with scientific personnel for the computer industry, will consider undergraduate registrants. Professional and Executive Recruitment (PER) was previously operated through the Training Agency but is now a private recruitment consultancy with offices throughout the country. Check your local telephone directory.

## Individual organisations/Professional bodies

It is common practice for jobs to be advertised internally before any external advertisement appears. The BBC and many other public service organisations, including educational ones in this country and overseas, operate in this way. Knowing someone who works for such an organisation, or having a vacation job with one, can be a way of obtaining advance knowledge of such vacancies.

## Personal contacts

Family, friends, academic staff, previous work or consulting research colleagues or acquaintances might all be possible sources of information about jobs. Don't be reticent about consulting such contacts. True, some people want to 'make it on their own'. Others realise the potential help available through such contacts. An increasing number of women are establishing 'Network Groups'. These might be for workers in a particular area – Women in Banking, Women in Media, Women in Youth Training, Association of Women Solicitors, Women in Electronics – or broader groups such as the National Organisation for Women's Management Education. Many of the books included in the further reading lists include information about such groups.

## Personal advertisements

Following up advertisements in personal columns, or placing them yourself, *can* be a good way of getting a job. It *can* be a recipe for disaster too. Use your common sense. Use initials: A Smith not Amanda Smith. Always use a box number rather than a private address. You can't be too careful.

## Press stories

News about someone's promotion, a new plant or superstore opening, takeovers, expansion plans, a huge order obtained, these and similar stories may mean possible openings for you. Use the speculative approach with your CV (see pages 53-4), and a brief letter referring to the press story.

## Luck

Certainly luck plays a part in jobhunting. Closer analysis of most experiences which are described as 'good luck' shows that in a lot of cases it is a matter of making your own luck, not only of being in the right place at the right time but also of making sure everyone knew you were around and interested.

## Further reading

*The Daily Telegraph Recruitment Handbook* (1990), London, Kogan Page (includes a directory of recruitment agencies and consultancies).

Smith, K and Associates (1986), *Women, Work and Training: A Manual of Training Resources for Use with Men and Women* (a supplement to the 1984 edition, containing an extensive network list), Sheffield, Manpower Services Commission.

University of London Careers Advisory Service (1989), *The Graduates' Guide to Recruitment Consultancies*, London, ULCAS.

Vacation Work Publications, Oxford, produce several guides to opportunities overseas, eg *Directory of Jobs and Careers Abroad, Work Your Way Around the World, Kibbutz Volunteer, Working in Ski Resorts*.

*Chapter 4*

# Put Yourself Across in Writing

## The application form

Jobhunting is an activity which has certain rules and conventions. The common analogy with a game is a good one. There is much to be gained from learning and understanding the rules, but much is unwritten and sometimes the rules change. Graduate recruitment abounds with myths, apocryphal stories and mystery. Yet there is only one route to a job, or indeed a postgraduate course. First, you sell yourself effectively on paper – the application form. Second, you talk about yourself – the interview.

Application forms set the scene for interviews. It is especially important to appreciate the rather obvious point that employers are not psychic; they cannot know something about you that you have failed to mention, be it through oversight, a failure to appreciate its relevance or false modesty. If you do not tell an employer about that second year survey of the local homeless, or that you learnt Japanese from scratch in the first vacation, or that you organised the most successful rag that anyone can remember, or captained the 3rd XI, or spent six months working your way round Australia between school and college etc, how on earth can she or he be expected to take them into account when assessing your capabilities and gauging what makes you tick? It is therefore time well spent to plan very carefully what you will say. Ideas are more likely to occur to you in the bath, on the bus or at the bar, for instance, than they are if you say, 'tonight at 8 I'll sit down and complete the form'. So, at the start of your jobhunting, get into the habit of jotting down thoughts as they occur so that you stand a better chance of remembering every piece of relevant information, all the evidence of your suitability for a particular job function. Project yourself as a credible candidate in your chosen field. This will involve getting ideas out of your head and into action. Announcing 'I want to be a journalist' is all very well as a vague aspiration but what have you done about it, what have you written, was it published, how varied is your style and what evidence have you that you can work under pressure and to deadlines, and so on?

Applications vary in style and length. They seek factual information about you, your educational background, and relevant work and other experience. They set the scene for the interview so you can predict at least some of the questions you will have to elaborate if you pass this first hurdle. Some of the more common questions are included in the Standard Application Form which is reprinted, with suggestions for completing it, on pages 43–8. Other forms can include far more 'open-ended' questions and it is these that cause so much anguish and apprehension:

What has been your greatest achievement to date?
What would not have happened were it not for you?
Where do you see yourself in five (or ten) years' time?
What are your main strengths and weaknesses?
And many more!

Most application forms include at least one question of this type.

Everyone is daunted by application forms. Some of the initial fear can be diffused if you realise why certain questions are being asked and then think how your own answers might be interpreted and plan accordingly. Women face particular difficulties here.

Many prejudices, assumptions and stereotypes affect the selection process. When thinking about your application form it is important to realise that, despite the Sex Discrimination Act and the efforts of the Equal Opportunities Commission in particular to ensure non-discriminatory advertising and recruitment practices, many employers continue to include questions about marital status and even number and ages of children on their application forms. Prejudices being what they are, such questions can set the scene for discrimination at the pre-selection stage. Of course, discrimination does not always follow, but there is a chance that thoughts such as these may cross a selector's mind: 'Thirty, married, no children? Won't be with us for long then', or 'Two children under five? She won't be able to cope with our hours', or 'Living in Birmingham, applying for a job in Newcastle? Marriage must be on the rocks', or 'Engaged? Better check what the fiancé's doing'. These and countless other assumptions can distort the recruitment process and in effect discriminate against female applicants. Although common sense tells you that most pre-selectors and interviewers will have partners and maybe children of their own (some of them even graduate jobhunters just like you), and that they will each have their own view about women at work, what you do not know is what that view is and how it will affect your application. Even if an employer is scrupulously fair, female applicants can face an extra burden of worry wondering whether and how they will be discriminated against. This extra burden is unfair and one which few men experience or understand. This book aims to help you to deal with some of the situations that arise from this situation.

If you noted some of the suggestions made in Chapter 2 you will remember the importance of self-evaluation and self-esteem. Have you noticed how it is somehow 'not British' to talk about ourselves in a very positive way? This way of looking at ourselves contrasts with, for example, the American tendency to emphasise the good points. Of course, such cultural differences have to be taken into account by international employers, and indeed by recruiters from ethnic minorities (see page 67). Another consideration is the considerable body of research which shows that women in particular are often reluctant to speak positively about themselves. 'It was luck', 'It wasn't anything important really', 'I think I might be able to', 'No one else would do it' are common phrases which display a lack of confidence. There is also a tendency to describe experiences in terms of the 'the supportive little woman' stereotype which is fine if that is what you are and want to remain, but should be avoided if you have other aspirations. Remember, you have to blow your own trumpet when jobhunting: no one else can do it for you.

## *Recognise your skills*

Think about those *skills which all students have.* You may already have noticed that the words 'previous relevant experience' often appear in job advertisements. They frequently put people off, students especially. There is a lot to be said for considering what lies behind these three words because anyone who has been through the higher education system in this country can claim some, if not all, of the following experience, much of which may be relevant. Look over this list whenever you feel despondent about jobhunting. It should give a boost to your morale and will help you to deal more effectively with application forms:

- *Work independently.*
- *Self-reliant.*
- *Effective planning of time.*
- *Work under pressure/to deadlines.*
- *Work unusual/erratic hours.*
- *Read vast amounts of material.*
- *Able to present information in an appropriate form* (long/

short essay, laboratory report, seminar paper, tutorial discussion, timed examination, maybe a speech/talk etc).

- *Able to synthesise, analyse, summarise material in cogent form.*

- *Can question/probe/give and receive constructive criticism.*

- *Developed skills in problem-solving, logical thinking, lateral thinking.*

- *Can exercise initiative.*

- *Can articulate thoughts and ideas verbally and in written forms.*

- *Able to adapt to different situations.*

PLUS perhaps:

- *Organised.*

- *Taken responsibility for others besides yourself.*

- *Socialised* (through vacation and other work experience, unpaid as well as paid, *know how to work with others*).

- *Gained an insight into management problems.*

- *Increased knowledge about the world of work* (and the society we live in).

- *Shown a willingness to care* (and do something outside the self and academic life).

- *Motivated others.*

- *Made things happen.*

- *Developed good communication skills.*

In other words you have developed that certain something, the 'personality' so often sought by employers.

More words and phrases litter the pages of recruitment literature. Here is a selection. Get used to them and practise using them to describe yourself.

| | |
|---|---|
| *drive* | *flexibility* |
| *resilience* | *thinking on one's feet* |
| *determination* | *ambition* |
| *originality* | *self-knowledge* |
| *sense of humour* | *persistence* |
| *responsibility* | *sociability* |
| *energy* | *resourcefulness* |

| | |
|---|---|
| *patience* | *risk-taking* |
| *motivate* | *intelligence* |
| *project* | *co-operation* |
| *promote* | *imagination* |
| *quick assimilation of information* | *sell* |
| *perceptiveness* | *creativity* |

Use phrases such as:

I *led*
I *developed*
I *managed*
I *was responsible for*
I *created.*

Always find a way of saying *because of my efforts X happened.*

Your use of such words and phrases will draw you to the attention of an employer and in a competitive situation this is what you will need to do. The words are not exclusive to industrial or commercial employers. The public service and charitable organisations, for example, are just as likely to use them because they too need the best possible staff in all areas. It therefore follows that it is the purpose/philosophy/political stance of the employer that decides the purpose for which the skills are used. You will need to think about this purpose when choosing which employers to approach. You should have the employer's recruitment literature in which you will find several clues about the adjectives you might most appropriately use to describe the skills you possess, and to demonstrate that you should be interviewed.

Employers are paying increasing attention to *personal transferable* skills. In a survey conducted in 1985 for the Standing Conference of Employers of Graduates (since re-named the Association of Graduate Recruiters) the following skills were highlighted:

identify problems/pose solutions
work in teams
communicate effectively in speech and writing
numeracy
adaptability.

Other skills mentioned were:

creative thinking
ability to relate to a wider range of people

management potential
leadership qualities
general social skills
self-management (set and achieve challenging goals, work
   under pressure, work to deadlines, self-motivation).

In a report (1986) which comments on employers' requirements of
the education system, the National Advisory Body for Public Sector
Higher Education added:

> the importance of extra-curricular activities – political, cultural or
> sporting – in developing leadership and teamwork skills should not
> be overlooked and all students should be encouraged to participate in
> such activities. Personal skills are highly valued in employment and
> there is dissatisfaction with candidates' capabilities in these areas.

In many cases it is not that the candidates lack capabilities but that
they have failed to tell employers that they have them.

Of course, some individuals put us all to shame by the amount
they seem to have crammed into their lives. That cannot be altered
and we could not become them even if we wanted to. What *can* be
altered however, is *your* attitude to yourself. The ingenious ways in
which you perceive and then describe your life experience to date
can certainly affect your chances of getting where you want to be.
So, think about and then list all the things that have happened to
you so far. Practise describing these experiences in positive terms,
and eventually 'translate' this into jobhunting jargon. Older
jobhunters have even more scope to develop this approach. You'll
surprise yourself once you re-interpret your past in this way.

When you have looked through several application forms and
drafted answers to some of the open-ended questions, you may
notice the underlying assumption in contemporary recruitment literature, and indeed the whole jargon of jobhunting, that there is
only one way to 'get on' and that is to say and do things the male
way. This topic is covered in much more detail in Chapter 6. Of
course, you will have your personal views about this, and the eventual decision about how you tackle forms is entirely your own.

Application forms are *not* the medium for reform, however. 'Why
aren't there any women partners?' looks rather aggressive on paper.
It might be more politic to wait for the interview when you could
say, 'I've read quite a lot about your organisation and it appears that
so far women have only reached the lower ranks of management.
Do you expect this to change?' or 'Are there any special management development schemes for women? I really want to get on.'
However, your real opportunity to change things is more likely to
come once you are in a job.

Recruiters are very busy people. Pre-selection (drawing up a short list for the interview on the basis of application forms) is undertaken quickly and often against previously determined criteria. Evidence that a candidate has failed to pick up clues and cues from recruitment brochures, job descriptions, videos etc about the culture of a particular organisation, and about the general jargon of jobhunting, means her application is heading for the reject pile. Harsh but true.

You should also realise that in a competitive situation, many employers use their recruitment brochures, the further particulars they supply on request, and application forms to put off unsuitable candidates and thus reduce the size of the postbag and the time taken to pre-select. Obviously you should take note of job specifications and requirements but they can be interpreted more widely than you might think. Degree titles can be a type of coded message in advertisements. While you could not apply for a job as a civil engineer with a degree in history, you might apply for a job in personnel with a degree in psychology if you wrote 'I notice that you specify "business studies" in your advertisement. I am reading psychology but in my second year I undertook a project on "implementing a training programme". This involved interviewing several personnel officers in local firms. This project (for which I got a First) taught me a lot about personnel work and several of the people I interviewed commented that I would be suited to this work. I hope that my application can be considered.' So, when you read advertisements, read between the lines; don't necessarily take the implicit no for an answer. If you have most of the skills and qualifications listed and really feel you are a strong candidate, then by all means have a go.

Occasionally employers ask you to attach a passport size photograph to your application form. This is usually to help the person who interviews you to distinguish you from the other 10 or 12 candidates seen on the same day.

## Hints on the Standard Application Form

What follows is an example of the way in which some of the questions which appear on the Standard Application Form might be answered, or some points to bear in mind when dealing with them. The example uses an undergraduate applying for her first job but it could be adapted to suit other circumstances. Fill in every box, even if only to say 'not applicable'. Forms frequently include a series of questions about ethnic origin and disability so that employers can monitor their equal opportunities policies.

# Standard Application Form (SAF)

AGCAS/AGR approved form

Please complete this form in BLACK ink or typescript.
Check employer literature or vacancy information for correct application procedure

Always follow these instructions

Current/Most Recent University/Polytechnic/College

First names (BLOCK LETTERS)

Out of Term address (BLOCK LETTERS); give dates at this address

Postcode                    Telephone

| Date of birth | Age | Country of birth | From | To |
|---|---|---|---|---|
| | | | | |

See chapter 7 for advice to mature candidates.

## Secondary/Further Education

Name(s) of School(s)/College(s)

# Name of Employer

Spell it correctly! No abbreviations.

Vacancies or training schemes for which you wish to apply

Job function(s)                    Location(s)

You can mention more than one function. To avoid accusations of woolly-thinking you can add 'At my interview I should like to discuss which would be most suited to my skills'.

Surname (Dr, Mr, Mrs, Miss, Ms) (BLOCK LETTERS)

Choice of title is often asked. You must answer it.

Term address (BLOCK LETTERS); give dates at this address

Try to give a number where an urgent message could be left.

Postcode                    Telephone

Nationality/Citizenship | Do you need a work permit to take up employment in the UK?

If you do not need a work permit but your name may make someone assume you do, it is sensible to put 'No, my family has lived in the UK for 40 years', for example.

Subject/courses studied and level (eg O, GCSE, A, H, ONC, BTEC)
Give examination results with grades and dates

No need to put failures unless you are specifically asked, or unless omission leaves a gap in the record. Be positive: 'Having failed O level/GCSE maths, I was determined to retake so I got a temporary job (see next page) and studied at evening class.

## First degree/diploma

University/Polytechnic/College

| | From | To | Degree/diploma (BA, HND, etc) | Class expected/ obtained | Title of degree/diploma course |
|---|---|---|---|---|---|
| | | | | Be optimistic | No abbreviations. Remember one-third of jobs advertised are open irrespective of discipline. |

Main subjects with examination results or course grades to date, if known

List all options even if technical in nature. Include subsidiary subjects, any projects. If no results given until final exams, say so. If some options are particularly relevant to the job applied for, these could be mentioned first.

## Postgraduate qualifications

University/Polytechnic/College

Put 'not applicable' if you are an undergraduate.

| | From | To | PhD/MA/ Diploma etc | Title of research topic or course |
|---|---|---|---|---|
| | | | | Give exact title. Put 'not applicable' if you are an undergraduate. |
| | | | | Supervisor: Give full title: Professor A B Smith, PhD, FRS |

Detail any scholarships, awards or prizes won at School and University/Polytechnic/College

If your school etc did not give prizes say 'None awarded by . . .'
If you've achieved Duke of Edinburgh's Gold, say so here.

Describe any aspect of your course of particular interest to you and/or of relevance to your application

Highlight topics that indicate you have certain skills required for the job applied for, eg 'During the third term of my second year and the summer vacation, I had to undertake a project. I chose to investigate the operation of the Youth Training Scheme in my local area. This involved devising a survey, talking informally, then using an interview questionnaire with instructors and YTS youngsters, analysing results and writing a 10,000 word report, with statistical tables, references etc. This was hard work but I enjoyed it. It was all worthwhile as I got a First, which counts as one-tenth of my degree.'

Any other qualifications/skills, eg knowledge of foreign languages (indicate proficiency), keyboard skills, computer literacy.

eg 'Good conversational French (I visit friends in Paris whenever I can), held clean driving licence for three years, attended evening classes in car maintenance in my first year, speedy two-finger typing, computer literate (I have my own small computer).'

Current driving licence?    Yes    No

## Activities and Interests

Give details of your main extra curricular activities and interests to date. What have you contributed and what have you got out of them? Mention any posts of responsibility

A very important question for aspiring managers. Only one person can be president of the Students' Union each year but there are other opportunities for responsibility/leadership/involvement/making things happen. Eg 'Member of six-member Staff-Student Departmental Committee: in the past year we negotiated a change in options, following a survey. I was chosen as chief negotiator.'

Mention things such as attendance at CRAC 'Insight into Management' course.

'Swimming four to five times a week for half an hour: my gesture towards keeping fit' sounds a bit more interesting than 'Swimming'.

Never lie and mention unusual hobbies – it will be your luck to be interviewed by an avid fan!

'Events Secretary, Industrial Society. Elected. I like to make things happen. I'm rather bossy but I hope in a nice way – people seem quite happy to follow my lead.'

'Volunteer Co-ordinator, Community Action Group. Uncontested post. Needs a clear head and good organisation. Huge satisfaction from matching volunteers to projects and from meeting so many people on and off campus.'

'Reading. Try to keep abreast of current affairs. Am working my way through the Virago list but would take the latest popular novel for holiday reading.'

# Work Experience

| Name of employer | From | To | Type of work, including sandwich placements, vacation and part-time work. Include voluntary work. |
|---|---|---|---|
|  |  |  |  |
|  |  |  |  |
|  |  |  |  |

Ideally you should have planned ahead and obtained some work experience, but if not . . . use this space in any way you wish. Be determined to show that you have had some experience of life outside educational establishments. At the very least, visit some local employers. Do remember that ALL experience is relevant in some respects and that in this context voluntary work as well as paid work counts. If you have never worked, explain how you spent that gift of time, the summer vacation, eg 'travelled round Europe on an Inter-Rail card'; 'took an intensive Teaching English as a Foriegn Language course'; 'appendicitis spoiled plans in 1989 – something (true) to fill the gap. If you were expected to complete an academic project in the vacation, say so. If you have had a lot of work experience this space will be too small so use a continuation sheet.

Which parts of this experience were most beneficial to you, and why?

Emphasise knowledge of self and knowledge of working environments. Eg

'Clerk, local hospital: developed my numerical skills and learned how to use a word processor, devised a new indexing system for patients' records.'

'Factory helper, pea-canning: work itself was monotonous but I learnt a lot about camaraderie among staff and the importance of management giving clear instructions.'

'Windsurfing instructor, Tahiti Plage, St Tropez: marvellous to be paid to do something I enjoy. Great satisfaction from seeing people of all ages improve as a result of my lessons.'

'Sales assistant, department store: had to take on more responsibility than most temps due to unexpected illness in my section (Ladies' Separates). Really got to know the business. Confirmed my choice of career.'

3

# Career choice

Explain what attracts you about the type(s) of work for which you are applying and offer evidence of your suitability

Avoid hackneyed phrases such as 'I want to work with people' (what sort of people, in what capacity?) and words such as 'helping' (who?) and 'interesting' (why?). Check the recruitment brochure for this employer's favourite words and phrases and use at least some of those. Eg

'My long-term aim is to run my own financial consultancy business. I have chosen accountancy training because this would give me a thorough business training, a professional qualification and eventually an opportunity to specialise. My 1989 summer vacation job and my third year project are evidence of my organisational and communication skills. I get satisfaction from doing a job well. I can relate to a wide range of people and am a loyal and supportive colleague. My experience on a group project in Year 1, and in dividing up tasks in my mixed flat in Year 3, have given me a 'feel' for working in a team, but I can work on my own effectively too (see section on vacation experience).'

## Please mention any points you wish to raise at interview

Broadly speaking, anything that is included, or omitted, from the brochure is fair game for a question but concentrate on career development and training issues rather than holidays/pension schemes/sports facilities. Eg

'I am especially interested in computer graphics, and once read an article which said your firm was a pioneer in this field, but it isn't mentioned in your Graduate Recruitment Brochure. Would there be any chance of working in this area?'

'Your brochure includes two biographies of staff who spent six-month secondments overseas within three years of joining. What opportunities might there be to use my language skills, once qualified?'

'Several of the graduates featured in your brochure have changed from their original job function choice. How common is this? I find the idea of change attractive as I want a varied career.'

## Do you have any restrictions on geographical mobility and/or a strong preference for a particular location? If so, give details

I am willing to work anywhere in the UK but would prefer the North West if a suitable vacancy is available.

If you feel there is anything which has not been covered adequately elsewhere on your application, please elaborate below. You could elaborate on a project or vacation experience.

Not everyone has had problems of crisis proportions but this space provides another chance to sell yourself. Relatively ordinary happenings can be included: 'My most significant difficulty overcome was leaving a close-knit family and moving 200 miles away but I adapted quickly.' And on to the more dramatic: 'My mother had cancer diagnosed two weeks before my A levels; despite the shock, I was even more determined to succeed as she had always encouraged me to study.' (This could be 'My mother had incurable cancer diagnosed as I took A levels so I decided to delay entering HE to help nurse her; she died the following February.')

Eg 'In the sixth form I wondered whether to try for the A level entry scheme you run. I applied in April 1988 although I had an unconditional place at . . . I withdrew my application after first interview because the person I saw (Mrs Brown?) said there would be another chance after graduation. I am very glad I followed her advice.'

| | |
|---|---|
| Have you any family connection or other contact with this organization? If so give details | Health matters of possible relevance – colour blindness, etc. |
| Eg 'My mother worked in your Accounts Department, 1962–1968' or 'not applicable'. | 'I suffer from . . . which is under control and my doctor assures me there will be no problems in pursuing my chosen career.' |

| Dates not available for interview | Date available for employment |
|---|---|
| During Finals . . . to . . incl. | Any time after 1 July but I understand your training programme usually begins on 1 September which I would prefer. |

Referees, one of whom should be academic. Give name, address and occupation (BLOCK LETTERS)
Do seek their permission first and tell them your plans so they can write more effectively about you.

**1**

DR MARY SMITH (PERSONAL TUTOR)
DEPARMENT OF

| Postcode | Telephone |
|---|---|

**2**

MRS JANE BROWN (PERSONNEL OFFICER)
BLOGGS & CO

| Postcode | Telephone |
|---|---|

| Date | Signature | Don't forget to sign. |
|---|---|---|

NB The Standard Application Form is constantly under review. Check with your careers service for the latest version.

## The CV and speculative approaches

Once you begin serious jobhunting you will notice that many employers do not mention application forms in their advertisements. 'Apply with full details' or 'Apply in writing, enclosing a CV' may appear instead. CV is the abbreviation of *curriculum vitae* (the literal Latin translation is 'the course of life'). There are many, often contradictory, views about the style, content, order and length of CVs. There is universal agreement about their aim. Your CV provides the means by which you project/sell/promote/advertise yourself so the reader wants to meet you.

### The main features of a CV

- Full name
- Full address and telephone number (give term-time address and dates if you are still a student)
- Date of birth/age/marital status/nationality (usually given but optional, could depend on the type of job applied for and/or your views about the relevance of such information)
- Education and qualifications (you do not have to give examination results but make sure all dates are accounted for)
- Other qualifications and skills
- Positions of responsibility held
- Work experience (mention most recent employers first)
- Interests and activities (if any of these are relevant to the job you are applying for, mention them first)
- Name, title and full address of two referees (usually a current or past employer and an academic tutor).

This information should be typed on plain white paper, A4 size. Only in exceptional circumstances should it be more than two sides long. Be careful about layout and spacing; make it clear and attractive for the reader. The style may vary depending on your chosen work area; what might be appropriate for jobs in the media might be suitable for applications for articled clerkships, for example. As with application forms, it is relatively easy to present facts in a positive way without resorting to lies or leaving unaccounted for time on your CV (failed A level, transferred course, unemployment can all be covered in this way).

If you thought that the Standard Application Form was hard enough, many other forms present additional difficulties, especially for women. An example follows. Such a form would be used for experienced applicants as well as new graduates. Occasionally forms are simple and offer minimal space for full answers to questions, in which case you will need to attach a carefully worded covering letter to fill in the gaps and ensure that you stand out in the crowd.

| Name in full | Business telephone number |
|---|---|
| Private address _____ <br> _____ <br> Telephone number _____ | How long have you lived at your present address? <br><br> How long did you live at your previous address? |
| Date of birth <br> Place of birth <br> Nationality | Single  Engaged <br> Married  Divorced  Separated <br> No. of children |
| Spouse's name <br> Spouse's occupation <br> Spouse's age | Name and address of spouse's employers _____ <br> _____ <br> _____ <br> _____ |
| Children's names and ages | What is your height?              ft.         ins <br><br> What is your weight in <br> indoor clothes?              st.         lbs |

Have you had any serious illnesses or do you have any physical handicaps? If so, give details

What is your present state of health? (N.B. in accordance with the regulations of the Society's Superannuation Fund, any appointment made would be subject to the candidate's passing a satisfactory medical examination.)

Is your sight good?                              Is your hearing good?

**Education**

| Name of School, College, University or Training Course | From | To | Full or Part-time | List Subjects passed, CSE, 'O', 'A' level etc., grades obtained and date obtained |
|---|---|---|---|---|
|  |  |  |  |  |

Are you currently pursuing a course of study? If so, give details

| What are your hobbies and pastimes? | Any special activities, clubs etc. <br> At school, <br> At University College, <br> After? |
|---|---|

**Employment**

| By whom employed and nature of business | From | To | Starting Salary | Job description and reason for leaving Salary on leaving |
|---|---|---|---|---|
| | | | | |
| | | | | |
| | | | | |
| | | | | |
| | | | | |

Are you currently, either, repaying a mortgage –          if yes:

Or if not, are you          With whom?

Type

paying rent?          Amount outstanding

living with relatives?          Rate of interest

Would you have problems moving if it were necessary?

Would you be prepared to move in furtherance of your career?

Give the names, addresses and occupations of your employer and one other person of whom enquiry may be made as to your character and abilities. (**We will not approach your current employer without your consent.**)

1. _____          2. _____
   _____             _____
   _____             _____
   _____             _____

Banker's name and address _____          Do you hold a current U.K. driving licence?

Give dates and details of all convictions or impending prosecutions for motoring offences. If none, insert 'None'

| Do you have any knowledge of: | Is your knowledge: |
|---|---|
| Group pensions | Very good/good/average/fair/poor |
| Individual pension arrangements | Very good/good/average/fair/poor |
| Self-employed pensions | Very good/good/average/fair/poor |
| Mortgages | Very good/good/average/fair/poor |
| Tax planning and Bonds | Very good/good/average/fair/poor |

When would you be free to take up any position offered?          What is the most important thing you expect from an employer?

Please write a brief biography. indicating whta you believe are your main achievements to date and what your aims are for the future.

Describe your current job in some detail. Additional space is available overleaf.

Why do you think you should get this job? What are your strongest qualities which fit you most for it?

Why do you wish to join . . . ?

New life business completed during past six years

| Year | No. of Pols. | Premium Income | Sums Assured | Year | No. of Pols. | Premium Income | Sums Assured |
|------|--------------|----------------|--------------|------|--------------|----------------|--------------|
| 19   |              |                |              | 19   |              |                |              |
| 19   |              |                |              | 19   |              |                |              |
| 19   |              |                |              | 19   |              |                |              |

What is your present salary?

Other benefits (e.g. car, expenses etc.)

Signature

Salary required

Date

Please attach a recent photograph of yourself to this Personal History.
N.B. Do **not** delay dispatch of this Personal History merely because you do not have a recent photograph readily available.

Opinions vary about the covering letter. Occasionally an advertisement states 'apply in writing', otherwise it is common practice to send a handwritten letter with a typed CV. Of course, your handwriting must be legible and good notepaper is essential. Always refer to the post applied for, when and where you saw the advertisement and state why you feel you are a suitable candidate.

## Speculative applications

CVs can be very useful when making speculative applications ie when a vacancy has not been advertised. (Note that some employers indicate in their *ROGET* entry whether such applications are considered.) Making your own luck can be an effective, interesting way of jobhunting as long as you are prepared to persevere and to use plenty of ingenuity in identifying possible employers to approach.

If you don't know whether a particular employer has vacancies but you know you would like to work for them you can approach them in three main ways.

### Telephone

Ask for whoever deals with recruitment and enquire whether there are any vacancies at present. At the very least you might be told 'we've nothing now but when we do we always advertise in the *Bloggshire Gazette* first'. Or you might be asked to send a CV which can be kept on file. Or you could ask for an appointment with someone working in the specialist area in which you are interested; such information-gathering often turns up likely sources of future vacancies, and provides useful points of contact.

### Letter

(a) Send your CV with a brief covering letter asking whether there are any vacancies for which you might be considered.

(b) Prepare a carefully worded letter addressed to the personnel officer by name if at all possible (you can get this from the switchboard operator in most cases). Provide full name, address and phone number. Explain why you are writing ('I saw in the *Gazette* that you are opening a new area office in Bloggstown. I am interested in a career in insurance sales and wonder whether you plan to take on additional staff in this area'). Outline your relevant experience and qualifications, emphasising what you have to offer. Indicate availability for interview, etc.

Or you could compromise between (a) and (b) by sending your CV with a covering letter in which you highlight and elaborate points which are particularly relevant.

## Other selection devices

Employers often use other devices in addition to forms and interviews in order to identify suitable candidates for their requirements. Such devices include aptitude/psychometric tests and biodata forms.

### *Aptitude tests*

The Civil Service and many parts of the computer industry have used a range of tests for many years. They are gaining popularity in other employment areas and as a jobhunter you should be aware of them.

Justification for the use of tests includes the belief that:

they can aid placement in specific job areas
they check basic levels of ability
they enable selectors to sift through large numbers of
    applications
they can provide information unavailable in an interview
they can test a hunch from an interview.

Tests are controversial among occupational psychologists and selectors as well as among jobhunters and their advisers. It is scarcely surprising that the enthusiasts are those whose own minds work in the way necessary to get a high score! However, like it or not, in order to get into certain types of employment you may well have to take a test. This fact may make you think twice about certain employers, but try to console yourself with the assurance given by selectors that test scores are but one of the many factors taken into account when their final decision is made and that for most jobs personal skills are important too. A few employers use a test in the first stages of recruitment and only those applicants who achieve an acceptable score are called for a first interview. Your own careers advisory service may be able to let you know the policies of regular graduate recruiters if such procedures are not mentioned in their literature or in the further particulars obtained in response to newspaper advertisements. However, tests more commonly form part of the procedures for second interviews (see pages 68–71).

If you want to learn more about tests and the justification for their use, consult the further reading list on pages 72–3 or look at the *aide-*

*mémoire* provided by British Telecom which helpfully explains their use of tests and provides a rebuttal of all the common objections to their use. If, after all that, your heart still sinks when you look at tests there is one solution – apply elsewhere. Never fall into the trap of believing those who say that women are no good at tests; most of them are very good indeed.

## Biodata forms

When employers have to deal with large numbers of applications for several job types and are anxious to save time and improve the match between vacancies and candidates and their staff retention rate, they may use biodata forms. These forms collect information about applicants in an impartial way and usually cover topics such as: background; education; work and other experience; and attitudes and values.

The forms have a multiple choice format. Usually they have been designed with a particular employer and/or range of jobs in mind. Apart from convenience for the recruiter they offer advantages to jobhunters too. There is objectivity and consistency – no worries about handwriting or whether yours is the first or fifty-first form the selector has seen that day. Speed is a big advantage. Filling in such a form might take you ten minutes instead of the two hours minimum required to complete effectively a more traditional application form with its inevitable 'essay' questions. There are two snags, however. One is that many student jobhunters, especially those without any previous work experience, find it difficult to say 'yes' or 'no' to questions when their natural response might be 'sometimes' or 'perhaps tomorrow but not today'. Another is dealing with natural suspicion. Most people get caught in a double-think trap when asked questions. 'If I say this they may think that.' Biodata forms provide agonising moments for experienced double-thinkers. Here are some examples:

- Typically, how do you prepare for examinations?
  (a) With a scheduled revision programme on all topics
  (b) Revision of weak areas over the last month or so
  (c) Prepare a few expected topics in depth
  (d) Crash revision in the last couple of weeks
  (e) None of these.

  (NB Careful planning and steady progress towards a goal are appropriate in some circumstances, but in others the creativity of the crisis of a looming deadline is crucial.)

- How many friends do you have?
  0–5 – up to 10 – 11–20 – so many I can't say

(NB In most societies, having friends is felt to be important but what does the word mean? Would acquaintances be more accurate? Some jobs require one to be gregarious but others might require a lot of isolation, or involve a close working relationship with a handful of people.)

Thus there are no 'right' and 'wrong' answers to biodata form questions, only inappropriate answers for particular circumstances. Given that most forms have up to 100 questions, you should accept that double-thinking is a waste of time and deal with the questions honestly. Incidentally, these forms do not always ask about marital status, age or ethnic origin, which excludes some potential areas of initial discrimination.

### Further reading

See Chapter 5, pages 72–3.

# Put Yourself Across Verbally

## The interview

One of the many ironies of selection as so commonly practised is that application forms often fail to project the applicant as she really is. Thus you could follow all the advice contained in this and other books, yet disappoint at the next stage – the interview. Similarly, in what are nowadays rather rare instances of automatic interview rather than pre-selection from forms, the candidate with an inadequate form might shine. Given numerous examples of these phenomena, it is scarcely surprising that a lot of luck is involved in interviews – what and who strikes the other person on the day.

You need to project yourself positively on the application form but not go over the top and turn yourself into someone else, a someone you have to pretend to be at the interview. Even if you successfully act your way through an interview it might prove hard to sustain the show for very long once you are in the post. Realistic honesty, giving yourself the benefit of the doubt, confidence in your potential based on evidence of past success is the best approach.

Interviews are imperfect methods of selecting the best people for jobs, yet human beings like to size each other up in this way. Occupational psychologists have considered this question for years. Even a glance at some of the books in the further reading section will show that opinions are sharply divided on this topic.

Given the inadequacy of the interview as an accurate predictor or identifier of the potential of an applicant in a given situation, ie the first job, it is scarcely surprising that there are other inadequacies too. Some of these inadequacies arise from assumptions, stereotypes and prejudices. It seems that no amount of training of interviewers will eliminate human foibles: 'Can't stand eye make-up', 'Handshake like a wet fish – weak', 'You can't beat a good old-fashioned girls' school', 'Keen windsurfer, just like me', 'Quite a charmer', 'Bit too keen on all this feminist nonsense'. 'Heavens, says her boyfriend will wait till she finds something before he starts jobhunting', 'Tiny thing, can't see her taking my lot in hand'. Such phrases are regular features of recruitment everywhere but remember that there are just as many comments about recruiters made by students and other jobhunters.

*Appearance at interviews*

A lot of men worry about this question, but more women do. Common sense is crucial. Even though you may be applying for a job in an area where you know casual or unusual clothing is common, it will pay to be reasonably conventional at an interview.

In *The Language of Clothes* Alison Lurie provides some fascinating views on the significance of our choice of clothing, or at least the significance that may be attached to it by others. Interviewers may not all have read this particular book but they will certainly be expecting certain things from you. In the case of traditional graduate employers it is expected that candidates will know that part of the jobhunting game involves dressing in a uniform. This uniform varies slightly: one year it is plain, usually grey, suits with demure white blouses; the next it might be tailored skirts, similar blouses, plus smart, co-ordinated jackets; the next, plain dresses. Some American research has shown that men are more likely to hire women who wear jackets at interviews. Be that as it may you have to show that you understand the form of code which says 'I know what is expected of people going to interviews. Their choice of clothing must show that they have taken the trouble to prepare themselves, externally and internally, for the ordeal ahead.' Some ordeal it can be too. Your clothes should relate to the profession or organisation you apply to join.

You may say that on no account do you want to dress this way, you haven't worn skirts since you left school and certainly don't intend to start now. If that is how you feel then that's fine but realise the implications of this. Like it or not, such strong views would eliminate many areas of employment. This may not seem fair but then the facts of jobhunting are harsh. And it may be comforting to know that there are other employers who do not mind about mode of dress as much as the more conventional ones, and indeed in some cases share opposite prejudices. Besides, there is always scope for compromise (not necessarily always the same as selling out). Thus you can dress up for the interview(s) and maybe during your training period too, but eventually you can apply for jobs in areas you find more congenial.

*So we've got you dressed, what next?*

- Plan where you have got to be and how you'll get there, and make reasonable time allowances. If you are early you can always walk around the block, or wait in the reception area reading suitable briefing material and exchange pleasantries with the receptionist who may well be asked for views about candidates later. If you are late the panic will place you at an immediate disadvantage. If you are unavoidably detained try to phone to apologise and give the approximate time of arrival so that your appointment might be exchanged with someone else's later in the day.

- Highly practical points are worth remembering too. Take an umbrella. Most women use handbags. Make sure yours contains some change (for that phone call) as well as a phone card, and means of meeting expenses if you are not refunded immediately. Comb. Tissues. The means to touch up your make-up if you use it. Small notepad and pencil. The card with your questions. Any testimonials or certificates you may have been asked to take. The letter asking you for interview. A copy of your application form. And do include your favoured sanitary protection as sometimes nature has an awkward way of displaying stress.

- Depending on the type of job applied for, it might be appropriate to take a folder containing samples of your written or art work. Occasionally employers ask for this beforehand.

- Develop a firm, but not vice-like, handshake.

- Look people in the eye.

- Try to pitch the voice so as not to become strident in argument or inaudible through nervousness.

- Smile, but don't giggle nervously.

- Many workplaces have no smoking policies so avoid smoking unless you discover that your interviewer is smoking and invites you to do the same.

- Be enthusiastic about the topics you've mentioned on your form as being of particular interest.

- Don't fidget. Practise sitting in a confident, semi-relaxed pose. Don't sit on the edge of the chair, wringing your hands, looking at the floor, crossing and uncrossing your legs every few minutes, chattering. If you manage to create an aura of confidence, even though you may be quaking inside, this will create a good impression.

The interview may seem fairly informal. Don't let that lull you into a false sense of security in which you divulge too much inappropriate information, or relax too much, or babble, or make the mistake of behaving as though the interviewer is a friend. Interviewers are usually trained professionals with a clear task, ie finding the most suitable candidate(s) for the job(s) available. They are not looking for friends, although some may be looking at you as a future colleague and, of course, colleagues can become friends. Research has shown that women make particularly tough interviewers so beware of the trap of thinking that all women interviewers you meet will be on your side.

Most, but not all, interviewers are trained. Most will know how to make you relax and get you talking, others will not. You may be reminded of that saying, 'do as I say not as I do' if you meet an ill-prepared or tactless interviewer or if you are kept waiting ages after the time announced for your interview. Interviewers do not always match the criteria laid down in their own recruitment literature. Occasionally they flirt and you will have to work out for yourself how to deal with that. Sometimes they don't seem to know as much about the job as you do. All of which goes to show that interviewers are only human too. They have colds, their families fall ill, their cars break down, they forget their papers. If any of these human foibles are apparent in any of your interviewers, make a sympathetic comment; it will be much appreciated.

During an interview most interviewers grade performance according to previously agreed criteria. The personnel/training department of a large organisation will try to ensure that its team of interviewers applies common standards as far as possible. The criteria will vary depending on the needs of particular jobs but there will be an agreed standard; everyone will know what they are looking for, what skills and qualities are required. Here is one example of guidelines for interviewers, adapted and reproduced with the kind permission of the Ford Motor Company Limited:

## *Characteristics likely to be found in successful candidates*

### SPECIAL APTITUDES
Candidate has special aptitudes, training or experience in:

- Bargaining, negotiation, persuading
- Problem analysis
- Organisation.

Candidate is numerate.

## INTELLIGENCE

- Very quick on the uptake
- Can handle questions which need analysis before answering
- Can demonstrate analytical reasoning and imaginative skills in discussion and problem-solving
- Can grasp and discuss abstract topics lucidly
- Where feasible, attempts to answer constructively
- Gives answers which are generally in touch with reality.

## DISPOSITION

- Has held responsible positions successfully (ie has taken actual leadership action, not merely held office)
- Has shown ability to influence people
- Stands up for herself/himself
- Record shows that what s/he undertakes s/he sees through
- Has shown initiative in dealing with problem situations
- Is aware of own strengths and weaknesses.

## MOTIVATION

- In decision-making situations, has generally taken all relevant factors into account and prioritised them sensibly
- Record shows that s/he systematically pursues success in both academic and non-academic pursuits
- Has set ambitious goals and appraised chances realistically
- Applications have a discernible pattern, eg looking for firms with a reputation for pay, conditions, training etc and the firms are mostly industrial
- Candidate willing to work in plant conditions
- Can state the things about Ford which make working for it attractive
- Has acquired information about, or experience in, chosen function
- Has reached university/polytechnic despite severe obstacles, eg bad school, antagonistic parent etc, and is coping with higher education
- Has had work experience. Can describe and evaluate what s/he learned about the operation on which s/he was employed, the relationship s/he formed with supervision and fellow workers
- Can relate work experience to career aims
- Has had some work experience above routine level.

*Interview questions*

As you saw in the section on application forms pages 37–42), you have already set the scene for your interview by what you have told the employer about yourself. Enough to make them interested, to make them want to know more. When preparing for your interview you should therefore remind yourself what you put on your form, and think about the various possible follow-up questions. Try putting yourself in the interviewer's place; there is a reasonable chance that at least some of the questions you anticipate in this way will be raised. For example:

Why a degree in X subject?
Why at Y institution?
With the benefit of hindsight, are you glad about the choice?
Tell me about this second year project you've mentioned.
I'm not a mathematician myself – whatever is topology?
I see your fourth A level was a much lower grade than the
    others; was there a reason for that?
What is the particular appeal of production management?

As preliminaries, however, you are more likely to be asked 'How are you today?' or 'How was the journey?'
  Other typical questions are:

Tell me about yourself.
Why this organisation?
Why do you think you would make a good marketing manager/
    public relations officer/arts administrator or. . . ?
What are your major strengths? (Be quietly confident.)
Why did you leave your previous job-course? (Never speak
    badly about former colleagues, teachers etc even if they were
    the main reason for your departure. This is because loyalty
    is felt to be an important attribute. It is better to answer pos-
    itively in terms of a fresh challenge, more appropriate
    course.)
Why should we offer this job to you? (This is sometimes asked
    after group interviews and you may well be asked which of
    the applicants you would choose were you on the selection
    panel. Do speak up for your own case but refer to the posi-
    tive qualities of other applicants too.)

Less usual questions are:

What is the most useful criticism you ever received? From
    whom?

But there are other sorts of question too, rather more searching:

> I see you've mentioned 'personnel' as your preferred job func-
> tion but your vacation work experience has been as an
> accounts clerk. What is the attraction of personnel?
> What would you say were your main weaknesses? (Remember
> that even faults can be described as attributes, thus 'I get
> very impatient with people who don't pull their weight'.)
> Now you've put down here 'staff-student liaison committee';
> what does that do and what happened while you were on it?
> (This is an example of a question that you can anticipate,
> and which should give you a chance to shine. What issues
> arose? How were they tackled? What changes resulted? Were
> you a reliable committee member? Did you make things
> happen? Did you deal tactfully with an awkward situation?
> Did you make any unpopular decisions? Did you represent
> the views and interests of your fellow students? And how did
> you feel in all these situations and what have you learnt
> from them? *You* are the expert on this particular topic. What
> the interviewer genuinely wants to discover is the answers to
> the questions because they will provide evidence of skills,
> aptitudes, self-knowledge, perceptiveness and so on, all of
> which are relevant in many work situations.)

Having had the opportunity to elaborate some points raised on the
form, it is likely that you will face at least one hypothetical question.
Such questions are designed to test whether you have thought about
what you might have to do were you to get the job, whether you have
taken the trouble to find out what to expect. Evidence of your prep-
aration for such questions might be a visit to local employers, talking
to people already working in your chosen field, reading around the
subject via the business pages of the newspapers, for example. The
questions will also test whether you can think sensibly on your feet,
how you might approach problems, how you would deal with colleagues.

Occasionally interviewers try to assess candidates' general
capabilities by using current affairs topics. Questions couched in
such terms are not seeking answers to such complex issues as the
Middle East conflict, global warming or poverty in the Third World.
They are designed to get you talking, to hear how you deal with
multi-faceted problems. They are not designed to trap you although
you may find that the interviewer adopts a 'devil's advocate' role for
a time, arguing against every point you make – again testing you for
certain skills in difficult situations.

If you do not understand a question, ask for clarification, or reflect the question back to the interviewer who might then realise you have been mislead. Silence can be effective and constructive, as long as you look as though you are thinking rather than being paralysed by nerves!

You can also pick up cues from body language. Do *they* look uncomfortable, interested, amused or bored? Do they make brief interjections (Hm . . . I see . . . Really . . .) which encourage you to continue talking? You can always let them off the hook and display your sensitivity if you say, 'Is that enough on that subject or would you like me to continue?'

## *Potentially difficult questions for women*

Interviews can be a minefield for women applicants, as they frequently face other questions which give an extra dimension to an already tense situation. A selection of such questions follows, an extract from 'Issues for Women Students'. Note that such questions and comments are contrary to the spirit, if not always the letter, of the law, in this case the Sex Discrimination Act. This fact does not stop these and other offputting questions being raised in all too many interviews, but it does give you certain rights. If you face any difficulties, do consult your own careers service or send details to the Equal Opportunities Commission.

● Married, I see. No doubt you will be leaving soon to have children?

If you are asked this type of question, do not be tempted to react angrily; rather be prepared to state calmly that having a family is a long way in the future, or to produce reasons why working and having a family are not mutually exclusive activities. (NB There is a huge change in employees within two to three years of graduation, no sign of different 'staying power' between the sexes at this stage, and no difference in absenteeism later. Don't be tempted to make statements such as, 'Oh no, I don't want kids'. It is not necessary to commit yourself in this way and even if it is true for you now, you may change your mind.)

● Live in London? Husband in the City? Can you claim to be fully mobile with three children under ten? How can you possibly look after them and work for us?

Say something positive and firm about your ability to manage your domestic affairs!

● How would you deal with male chauvinism on the shop floor?

● Engineering? Not a very female subject is it?

Try not to be put off by put-downs. Be firm and positive.

● Believe in equal opportunities eh? Don't tell me you're one of those awful women's libbers!

When faced with loaded questions of this type, much more is likely to be achieved in the way of changing attitudes if they are answered firmly but with tact and patience.

● We might not get a return on our investment if we appoint you rather than a man.

You might ask calmly how many men and how many women are still with the employer after three years. Emphasise evidence of your powers of persistence, 'stickability', determination to see things through.

● After a trainee joins us, he will. . .

Careless use of the male pronoun can be offputting. You could ask if this means that you will be the first female trainee.

● How numerate are you?

Maths may never have been your favourite subject, but don't underestimate your ability to deal with numerical information. Most employers are looking for a common-sense approach to figures, not a mathematical genius!

● Are you willing to be mobile?

You should have thought about this before applying but here is a chance to rethink. Don't be tempted to make promises you cannot keep.

● To be honest, we'd anticipated someone younger for this job.

Outline what you feel you have to offer and how your wider experience will be an advantage. The employer may assume that an older person will be less prepared to learn new skills or take directions from a younger person, so stress your adaptability.

● Where do you see yourself in ten years' time?

Where indeed! Employers are fond of this type of question. Concentrate on career development aspects – fulfilling potential etc – rather than personal matters.

If you feel you are being pushed into an awkward corner during an interview, especially over personal questions, it can be an effective tactic to try responding with another question. For example:

Q.  Are you married?

A.  Does your organisation have a preference?

It takes a lot of confidence and quick-wittedness to cope effectively in such situations.

### *Your questions*

Almost always you will be asked if you have any questions. This invitation is usually extended at the end of an interview when you feel time is running out. Do prepare some questions. Jot them down on a small card if you like; this tactic can have a calming effect, especially if your mind goes blank at the crucial moment, and it will make you look sensibly well prepared. Questions should concentrate on the job/training scheme, your initial training and eventual career development. You can ask about the proportion of women in senior management too if such information is not available elsewhere and if the answer will help you to make a decision if you have several job offers. If salary has not been mentioned before it is sensible to ask about it even if you introduce the subject by the ploy of 'money isn't everything but. . .'. Never argue about salary until you have a firm job offer – *then* you negotiate. Views differ about the advisability of questions on pensions, holidays, hours of work and other terms and conditions of service. For graduate management training schemes it is usually possible to obtain this information from the young trainees to whom you will be introduced during the selection process.

It is quite possible that all your questions will have been covered, in which case you can compliment the interviewer by saying: 'Well, I did have several but you have already covered them, thank you.' Never ask a question just for the sake of it.

### *The result*

In closing the interview, the interviewer should tell you when you can expect to hear the result. If not, ask. If you do not hear within a week or so of the predicted date, write or phone. At the very least this will indicate your enthusiasm and motivation and will keep your name in their minds. Any problems should be reported to your careers service. Remember, recruitment is a public relations exercise too. Even if an employer decides to reject you, you may be an influential customer later on and it is in their best interests to treat you well. See also The Job Offer, pages 71–2.

## Thank you letters and other correspondence

Opinion is divided on the question of thank you letters after interviews, which is common advice to jobhunters in the United States, for example. If your approach has been a speculative one, or you obtained an interview as a result of a personal contact, a thank you letter is more appropriate than in the more conventional jobhunting situation. Most people appreciate being thanked, however. If you have enjoyed an interview (yes, that is possible!) and your experience has made you even keener to join the organisation, writing to say so will do you no harm. Equally, if you have thought further about some of the issues raised at an interview and you wish to add comments, write. This can be particularly sensible if you were asked to consider job functions other than the one you specified on your application form. If you feel the interviewer did not allow you to put your case across effectively you could write a tactful supplementary letter – it is said that a good interviewer lets the candidate talk for at least 60 per cent of the time – but do seek advice on this first. As with any other business correspondence, use plain writing paper; leave those flowery or brightly coloured sheets for your friends.

## A note on telephone interviews

Occasionally initial interviews are conducted over the telephone. This is especially common for sales jobs where you might be involved in a lot of telephone work yourself and where you must be able to establish rapport, capture the attention of another person and get your message across quickly and effectively. Remember:

- have a copy of the advertisement to hand
- also your current CV in case your mind goes blank when asked factual questions about yourself
- plenty of coins and a phone card if you have to use a public telephone
- speak firmly but pleasantly, with no verbal mannerisms.

## Cultural differences and interviews

In the context of interviews it is relevant to mention that misunderstandings can arise for both interviewee and interviewer if one or other of them is from an ethnic minority group. Assumptions based on stereotyped expectations, varying opinions about what are and are not acceptable topics for discussion, attitudes to success or failure, lack of familiarity with the concept of hypothetical problems can all cause problems. Try talking this through with your careers adviser if you are worried about it.

## Second interviews

Many employers of graduates hold second interviews, as if the first stage was not difficult enough! Your 'reward' for success at that first hurdle is invariably a more searching/harrowing experience. What might happen?

### Simple

You are invited to attend an interview at a stated time and location. You will see at least one member of staff, who will possibly, but not invariably, be a future colleague. You might also be shown around the premises. You might have travelled 200 miles for an event which might last no more than an hour. Some extremely large and prestigious organisations still use this simple method as the second stage in their recruitment.

### Complicated   (and more usual among the regular large recruiters of graduates)

These may include some or all of the following:

1. An overnight stay at a hotel, or maybe at the organisation's training headquarters. You will be asked to assemble for drinks and dinner where you will meet graduate trainees and other staff. This may be followed by a talk about the organisation and what it has to offer.

2. Tests of various types (see page 54).

3. Give a talk either about yourself or on a general or specific topic.

4. Group exercises.

    Let's say six to eight people have been invited for second interview. The organisation wants to see how each of you behaves in a group so may use several different exercises, eg:

    • A series of topics may be given by the selectors and

you have to discuss each for a few minutes, eg student grants should be abolished; a woman's place is in the home.

- An 'in-tray' exercise, ie you are given an imaginary in-tray and asked to consider how to deal with the contents; you may have a few minutes to decide your own priorities first but then discuss them as a group.

- A case study, ie you are given a written description of a situation and asked to make recommendations for action. Again you would typically have some time to consider your own reactions before being asked to devise a group solution to the problem.

- A game of some sort, usually designed to test your powers of lateral thinking in problem-solving, eg being given a set of toy houses, trees, animals, roads etc and being asked to design an ideal community. (NB Although a touch of humour is always welcome do avoid the temptation to poke fun at the exercise itself – recruiters can be sensitive!)

Faced with such an array of possible ordeals how can you best prepare yourself? Apart from keeping as calm as you can – and avoiding over-indulgence the night before – there is relatively little you can do. You should be aware that the observers/ assessors involved in such exercises will be working through checklists of the positive and negative qualities demonstrated by each member of the group.

*Negative* qualities include:

silence (whether from acute shyness or failure to get a
  word in edgeways)
monopolising discussion
interrupting others
criticising others and/or putting them down
patronising or condescending attitude
aggressiveness
inability to accept criticism
stubbornly sticking to one point of view
ignoring what others say
red herrings.

*Positive* qualities include:

 making an early contribution
 keeping to the topic or task
 making constructive suggestions
 listening to others and building on their ideas
 getting others to talk
 a team approach to the task
 being aware of the time
 showing good humour
 accepting that some problems have a variety of solutions
     and that compromise is sometimes necessary.

Most employers say that during such exercises they are looking
for potential, for someone who is willing to have a go at tackling
a problem and who makes some visible progress during the
day. Talking the most and loudest, regardless of the behaviour
of other people, is not usually interpreted as being synonymous with having management potential.

5. Interviews

- One to one, possibly covering some of the same
  ground as in your first interview. A typical sequence is
  an interview with a personnel officer, then a line manager and/or someone from the department you would
  like to join or a specialist in your preferred job function.

- Panel interviews are more common in the public sector
  than elsewhere. As a general rule look most at the person who has asked the question, with occasional
  glances at the others to involve them. If you can
  remember names and refer to what they have said, so
  much the better.

If you pass all these hurdles, when you receive your job offer (see
pages 71–2) you might be invited to see the offices or laboratory in
the section of the organisation in which you will work. If such a visit
is not offered you are quite entitled to ask for one if you feel it will
help you to make up your mind. Of course, visits are normally built
into interview procedures but they are not always feasible, eg if the
second interview stage is held at the national training establishment
or a head office.

  You can reasonably expect that all travelling and other expenses
connected with interviews will be met by large employers; the practice

among smaller recruiters varies. If the letter asking you to interview does not mention this it is sensible to ask beforehand.

Take comfort from the fact that by the time you get to the second interview stage in the recruitment process you have a very good chance of success. Employers report that, proportionately, women do every bit as well as men and in some cases better.

*Note*: There is a Code of Practice which covers most aspects of selection procedures and outlines the obligations of employers, careers services and students. This Code has been negotiated by the National Union of Students, the Association of Graduate Careers Advisory Services and the Association of Graduate Recruiters. Copies are available from your careers service and the Code is reprinted in recruitment directories and other careers literature. If you feel that an employer is in any way infringing this Code, consult your careers adviser.

## The job offer

You may have to wait several days, or weeks, or in a few unfortunate cases months, before you hear the result of an interview. Always ask your interviewer when you might expect to hear.

The offer letter should indicate job title, location, starting date, salary and other terms and conditions of employment. It may state that this is subject to the receipt of satisfactory references and/or a medical examination. You may be asked to make a decision by a certain date. Don't rush this. You may want further information from the organisation, or want to wait to hear the results of other interviews. Or you may want to negotiate a different starting date. At least you have the satisfaction of knowing you are wanted, and that puts you in a powerful position.

If you are a final year student the Code of Practice establishes the convention that an employer should not force you to make a decision until the end of the Easter vacation. In reality this can cause difficulties for both employer and applicant so do discuss any problems with your careers adviser. Employers who belong to the Association of Graduate Recruiters which negotiates the Code are large, regular recruiters who are usually able to plan well ahead. Smaller employers who might have only a handful of vacancies each year and who advertise those as and when they need to recruit would not expect to be kept waiting for long if they made you an offer.

Accepting a job offer in writing means that you and the employer have entered a legal contract. Reneging on job offers is therefore an extremely serious matter.

If you have any doubts about accepting an offer consult as many people as you can but if you do not want to be rushed into a decision, for example, you can always withdraw with reasonable confidence knowing that if one employer wanted you others will too. There are no guarantees, however; you will have to take a gamble.

Occasionally employers allow graduates to defer entry for several months. Negotiating such a deal can be tricky. As a general rule it is best to raise the question once you've received a job offer. Some employers may ask you outright in your first or second interview in which case you can have a frank discussion while keeping your options open, eg 'I'm glad you've raised that point because I was wanting to ask you about the possibility of deferred entry. I've been asked to go to help in my aunt's business in Australia for a few months. It's a marvellous opportunity and I feel it would be useful in my future career. On the other hand, I don't want to miss out on a good job here. What do you think?' Large organisations occasionally agree to such plans.

Negotiating deferred entry in order to undertake postgraduate work can be far more difficult. Consult your careers adviser and academic staff. Some employers expect that the more academically brilliant students will want to do this anyway, or at least consider it an option. Others insist on earlier single-mindedness and could not be kept waiting until you knew that you had both a place and funding.

Having accepted a job offer the question of your *next* job is probably far from your mind. The fact remains that there is a high turnover of highly qualified staff in many organisations. The reasons for moves are many and various and need not concern you immediately, but you should realise that there is little or no question of you joining one employer for the whole of your career. This is no longer a common pattern of employment. By choice or circumstance there is far more movement between organisations. We now consider what might happen to you in that first job. What might lie ahead for you?

## Further reading for Chapters 4 and 5

Adams, S (1980), *Law at Work: Sex Discrimination*, London, Sweet and Maxwell.

Barrett, J and Williams, G (1990), *Test Your Own Aptitude*, London, Kogan Page.

Davidson, M (1985), *Reach for the Top*, London, Piatkus.

Equal Opportunities Commission (1982), *Code of Practice for the Elimination of Sex and Marriage Discrimination and the Promotion of Equality of Opportunity in Employment*, Manchester, EOC.

Equal Opportunities Commission (1985), *Application Forms Free of Sex Bias*, Manchester, EOC.

Herriot, P (1984), *Down From the Ivory Tower: Graduates and Their Jobs*, Chichester, John Wiley.

Hopson, B and Scally, M (1984), *Build Your Own Rainbow: A Workbook for Career and Life Management*, Leeds, Lifeskills Associates.

Josefowitz, N (1986), *Paths to Power*, London, Columbus Books.

Lurie, A (1983), *The Language of Clothes*, Feltham, Hamlyn.

National Advisory Body for Public Sector Higher Education (1986), *Transferable Personal Skills in Employment: The Contribution of Higher Education*, London.

Nierenbery, G and Calero H (1984), *How to Read a Person Like a Book*, Wellingborough, Thorsons.

Phillips, C (1987), *Coping with Job Hunting*, London, Newpoint.

Roberts, C (1985), *The Interview Game and How It's Played*, London, BBC Publications.

Roberts, M (1985), *What Employers Look for in their Graduate Recruits*, London (Standing Conference of Employers of Graduates).

Roizen, J and Jepson, M (1985), *Degrees for Jobs: Employer Expectations of Higher Education*, Guildford, SRHE and NFER-Nelson.

Skeats, J (1989), *Getting the Right Job*, Dorking, Templar.

Slaughter, A (1987), *Your Brilliant Career*, London, Macdonald Optima.

University of London Careers Advisory Service (1989), *How to Write a CV*, London, ULCAS.

There is a wealth of further information in careers advisory services including reports of interview procedures adopted by different employers. Especially useful are the AGCAS information booklets *Applications and Interviews* and *Jobhunting After Graduation*, and the Exploring Your Future Workbooks on *Making Applications* and *Going for Interviews*. The AGCAS videos are particularly helpful, covering all aspects of the jobhunting process – *Write, Giving Full Details, Tell Me, Mr Dunstone* and *Two Whole Days*.

## Chapter 6
# Look Ahead

**Women at work**

The 1990s will provide additional opportunities for women. The Institute for Employment Research at the University of Warwick has predicted that up to 1995 there will be about 1 million fewer young people available to employers, a drop of about a quarter. Meanwhile, it is expected that there will be an increase of women in employment, mainly those returning after a break for child-rearing, and these will fill the vast majority of the new jobs anticipated, most of which will be in professional and related occupations. Further evidence that the better one's qualifications, the better one's prospects.

So you've got that all-important first job. What challenges and conflicts might arise in your professional and personal life? Some of what follows is directed at the particular problems faced by women in managerial positions. Don't skip it. 'Management' is a term which is very loosely defined. Some people argue that the star manager of all is the housewife. Others associate management with long business lunches, heart attacks, having several too many at the Christmas 'do', tyranny or inadequacy, or a host of other characteristics which are based on unfortunate experiences and/or stereotypes, usually based on male managers. Yet good managers are needed in all work areas – charitable organisations, hospitals, publishing houses just as much as by oil companies, banks and car manufacturers. There is a desperate need for managers who show vision and flair, who will take responsibility for making things happen in their particular organisation.

Employers seek graduate recruits because proportionately more graduates have the intellectual and personal skills to become effective managers. As the proportion of women in higher education increases and as more women develop managerial career aspirations, inevitably more of them will enter management and in turn influence attitudes and approaches within the organisations for which they work.

Women are already making quite an impact. Increasingly, graduate recruiters comment that proportionately they see better-prepared and more effective female than male applicants. These graduates

74

will no doubt feature in articles and recruitment literature throughout the 1990s and will have the opportunity to progress further up
various hierarchies than their predecessors were able to do. This in
turn will offer more role models for other women. The figures
quoted in Appendix 1 indicating the current imbalance between
women and men in various work areas may look rather different by
the year 2000.

Of course, not everyone wants to be a manager. Nor are all
women keen to be pioneers, to enter the bastions of mining engineering, for example. Most women graduates think very carefully
about likely future colleagues and working environments. When
deciding on your preferred job function it may be useful for you to
know how many women staff particular employers have, and of
those, how many are in managerial positions. You may quite reasonably ask for information about the career paths of others; how they
were treated in terms of training opportunities, ordinary or extended
maternity leave, promotion or chances of career moves and changes
within the organisation, given that not everyone aspires to 'the top'
although it is good to know that that is a possibility. Several careers
guides provide helpful information on these and related topics. (See
pages 82–3.)

Women managers frequently face extra stresses and strains above
those which have always been associated with being a manager.
This is *not* to say that women cannot be very effective managers, just
that they often have to learn to cope with additional pressures to
those faced by their male colleagues. Cary Cooper and Marilyn
Davidson of the University of Manchester Institute of Science and
Technology have undertaken detailed research into this question
which all intending managers are advised to read.

Why might women face different pressures? Surely all managers
face stresses and strains? Yes indeed, but the Manchester research
has identified some specific potential and actual problem areas.
These areas include:

   high visibility
   feelings of isolation
   pressure to perform
   lack of confidence
   prejudice/patronising attitudes
   business travel
   entertainment
   sexual harassment (ie unwelcome sexual attention)
   home/work conflict (sometimes described as role overloading).

Being forewarned by reading about women in management and

talking to them can be very helpful. Several network and other groups exist which will enable you to do this. You may be put off the whole idea of a managerial career, or at least a managerial career in a male-dominated sphere. You may be fired with even greater determination to succeed whatever the odds and whatever the personal sacrifices along the way. You may indeed be determined to 'get in there and fight like a man'.

Behaving 'like a man', or thinking that this is necessary, can be one of the biggest traps of all for women. The next section considers why this is so and whether there are any alternatives to that commonly held view that assumes that the one way to 'succeed' is to behave like a (stereotyped) man. Most, but by no means all, women do not on any account want to forgo their (stereotyped) female traits. Perhaps instead of reinforcing a need to conform to a 'male' way of doing things, more women *and* men might be more comfortable if we emphasised differences. If there was greater emphasis on a gender-free approach to management, and indeed many other work and personal areas too, perhaps more people could be more effective in whatever role they happened to be in at the time. Thus men would no longer run the risk of being labelled 'soft' if they said they were keen to take a greater share in child-care, and women might not be labelled 'hard' if they aspired to a seat on the board.

You need to think carefully about some of these issues at an early stage in your jobhunting. This is not only because it is useful to clarify your own views but because it will help you to anticipate, deal with and probably also understand the views of others. This process will help you to realise the dangers of making assumptions – yours and those of others. Everyone has prejudices of one sort or another. Being aware of yours, and sorting out which are rational and which irrational in the context of careers choice and the application process, is vital.

What might these assumptions be? One concerns *competitiveness*. Books such as this are aimed at the individual. Were you to act on it there would be a good chance you would 'do better' than someone else who had never read such a book, discussed their plans with a careers adviser or indeed anyone else. You want that job or course place and it is obvious that if you are successful someone else may be disappointed. You are in a competitive situation and you have to play to win. The other sporting saying about 'it's the game that counts' is not applicable to jobhunting.

A lot of women don't like competition. Or is it that they don't like to admit that they are competitive? It is not part of the feminine stereotype for women to be seen to plan to get what they want in career terms although, of course, literature, music and theatre are full of stories of feminine wiles being used to win the attention of a man, or men! There is a contradiction here:

What about all those so-called romantic novels where Plain Jane with the lovely personality lands the Handsome Hero?
What about the TV ad 'heroine' with floors sparkling brighter than her neighbour's?
What about all those 'how to catch your man and keep him' articles in popular magazines?

Maybe women should be more honest with themselves about competition!

A trap that lies waiting for you if you don't accept any competitive traits in your character is that you might beaver away at your job, modestly accepting the occasional praise of your colleagues, or even your boss, and assuming that eventually your worth will be recognised. This passivity, or blind optimism, or sheer good nature, will get you absolutely nowhere. Numerous workplaces are full of hard-working, usually loyal, salt-of-the-earth people – men as well as women – who are overlooked in the promotion stakes, who exert energy which might be better spent elsewhere in moaning about their lot in life, who view with vehement jealousy the promotion of those of their colleagues they consider have none of their own attributes. Brenda Jones, in *Getting Ahead*, says:

You must accept responsibility for your own future, make opportunities for yourself, and increase your visibility within the organisation. If you don't have a clear idea of what you want from your career, you will just drift aimlessly or find yourself in a dead end.

If you don't make it clear that you are looking for promotion, that you have the necessary skills and motivation to 'get on', that you believe you can make your own luck, then you are in danger of becoming the proverbial doormat. Conscientiousness and loyalty are indeed virtues but not if you keep them to yourself.

It is sometimes said that women are not ambitious enough, that they are unwilling to make the necessary personal sacrifices in terms of reduced private life in order to make it to the top. Another way of looking at that might be to recognise that some women have decided that other parts of their lives are important to them and that their whole self-esteem is not vested in becoming partner, head, managing director, chief executive or whatever. As Natasha Josefowitz says:

Each individual discovers the amount of stress, responsibility, intrusion into personal time, that they can tolerate. In this case 'horizontal enrichment' can be a goal.

It is perhaps simplistic to describe this as lacking ambition.

Another assumption which can turn into a trap is that other women are automatically your friends or on your side. Research has shown that women are tougher on women in interview situations and that they do not always support each other at work (but neither do men!). Some women who have made very successful careers, but at considerable personal sacrifice and with very little help from others, occasionally feel that things are made too easy for young women these days. Such an attitude can be tinged with jealousy, of course, and the jealousy rears its head in many parts of the workplace as in other spheres of life. However, the enormous success of women's support groups of various types indicates that there are many women who *are* willing to share their experiences generously, to offer encouragement, support and advice. Consult the address list on page 112 and further reading lists throughout this book for more information on such groups.

In the past decade there has been a proliferation of 'career development' courses for both women and men. Such courses are run by individual consultants or under the auspices of the Training Agency (TECs), for example. (See page 33.) They are of varying length, cost and location. Their philosophies vary too. Sometimes they consider how to get the best out of self and colleagues, how to develop individual working styles, and to learn how to work together as people, not as women or men. This can lead to a more flexible approach to management, a move away from the scientific style of defined goals, target-setting and performance-orientation towards more variety and co-operation in reaching high standards. However, other courses adopt a much more traditional, tougher, stance. It is therefore sensible to enquire about the emphasis of any course before agreeing to attend.

## Positive action

Considerable attention has also been paid to the question of positive action for women. Topics such as under-achievement, under-representation, retraining, in-service training, management development, career and life planning have been discussed in numerous official reports, newspaper and magazine articles and several books. Excellent though such reports might be, they often represent the views of a few enlightened individuals in the personnel department or on the board perhaps, and do not always reflect the attitudes or behaviour of everyone in the organisation. Jobhunters should be aware of this and ask appropriate questions.

Positive action programmes received a boost in 1985 when the Equal Opportunities Commission issued a Code of Practice which is designed to advise employers about what steps they might take to ensure that they do not contravene the 1975 Sex Discrimination Act, and on how to introduce equal opportunity policies which might redress previous inequalities. Positive action programmes can apply to men, of course, although in practice they are mainly directed at women. They try to gauge what has happened in the past and to make recommendations on future action. These programmes tend to be much publicised. Local government, banks, television companies and universities are examples but there are many others, and large organisations are increasingly appointing 'equal opportunities officers' to establish such programmes. (See Appendix 2 for background to the legal aspect of positive action.)

It is self-evident that the better and more effective (however defined) the training given and the fairer the treatment received, the more satisfied an employee will be. It is therefore one thing to recruit you with all your personality and skills, but quite another to keep you. The fact that before too long you will be in a relatively strong position, that you will have considerable power, might not have occurred to you. Thinking about this power might help to boost your confidence. There are important public relations implications for many aspects of recruitment. If you are treated fairly, even as a rejected applicant, you will feel rather warmer towards the employer(s) – and the company's products or services perhaps – than if your application was greeted with disdain or ignored. Similarly, if you are well treated by your employer(s) you may decide to remain with them, an increasingly vital link in the management chain perhaps. Or you may be 'head-hunted' by a rival, but throughout the rest of your career you will say 'Smith & Co gave me my first chance, my basic training, I shall always be grateful to them', which gives them free advertising. Similarly, you may set up in business on your own, or be in a position to recommend other experts to your clients. People have long memories and many of them bear grudges as well as remember favours.

Women are still a minority in many work areas. You may be the first woman to have been appointed at a particular level. Of course, it is to be hoped that you discovered that this was to be the case during the recruitment procedure. Dealing with such 'pioneering' situations can be difficult but a lot of give and take, good humour and perseverance usually lead to acceptance and mutual understanding as, for example, many women industrial relations officers, distribution managers and site engineers will tell you.

## Women's management style

In recent years there has been increasing interest in a distinctive, female management style. Certainly there is recognition that women bring something different and generally beneficial to management situations. Consider the following extracts:

Women managers should stop pretending to be surrogate men. Instead, they should look at themselves and their own needs and then work out what they want from their careers.

(Judi Marshall)

. . . women show a greater willingness to look at leadership not as the role prerogative of the leader, but as the function best invested in several qualified people. The criticism brought against women who are said to avoid success and shun power may be better understood in terms of many women's preference for shared leadership, shared responsibilities, shared power. Does this come from affiliation needs, from the belief that two heads are better than one, from a lack of self-confidence, or from our wisdom about our own limitations and our ultimate concern that people and organisations will be better served by many than by one? Empowering others is empowering ourselves. Many women have learned that the collaborative mode fulfils organisational objectives effectively.

(Natasha Josefowitz)

Management style is often cited as an area where women have something special to give . . . It is said that they are accessible, sympathetic, informal, unstuffy, direct in getting to the point, not prone to stand on their dignity, realistic, concerned to get the best from people for the latter's own benefit as well as for the organisation's sake, spontaneous, honest, averse to wrangling, ready to 'grasp nettles' in human relations, brief in discussion. Of course, it is possible to think of examples of women who are not like this and of men who are. . . It seems obvious that one reason why women might be inclined to get to the point quickly. . .is that they have more to pack into the day than men. . . Men managers will extend the working day into the evening, knowing that when they get home there will be food, drink and warmth waiting. Women will long before that want to be away, seeing to the children's supper, doing some late shopping, preparing for husband's return, just ensuring that some family living takes place in the home as distinct from its being a mere depot for feeding, watering and sleep. . . Spinning out the working day encourages an undisciplined approach to work!

(Virginia Novarra)

Marshall argues that a female management style involves co-operation rather than competition.

Listening before acting; being sympathetic; being trustworthy; not needing to dominate others; getting things done by being nice to people; making friends with people so they try not to let you down; being

prepared to apologise if something goes wrong; being honest; showing respect and tolerance; listening and empathising.

Whatever personal management style a woman adopts she has to
understand the internal politics of an organisation. This has not
tended to appeal to women who often dismiss it as playing (male)
games. In many work situations women need to understand what is
going on because only then can they influence future events. You
will therefore need to bear this in mind when deciding how you will
deal with your work colleagues as well as social acquaintances and
friends. How you react to situations such as people assuming you
are a secretary when you answer the telephone or if you lead a negotiating team of men or if you attend a committee meeting. How you
cope with men who patronise or undermine you or taunt you with
sexist comments or generally undermine what may be – initially at
any rate – a precarious confidence. Once again, it is often the female
support systems that can come to the rescue in such difficult situations.
However, you will have to rely on your own judgement, tact and
empathy when dealing with your male colleagues' female partners
when you meet them in social situations as you may be perceived as
a threat.

You will also need to work out for yourself how to deal with the
question of dress. In the USA, dressing women executives is big business. There is every sign that this phenomenon will spread elsewhere,
with specialist designers and consultants and sections of high street
stores devoted to smart business suits with co-ordinated accessories.
Advertisers are also directing their attention to this market. Of
course, not all women managers dress in business suits. You will
have your own view on this and other aspects of particular jobs and
this will affect which employers you apply to; look around when
you go for interviews as people's work 'uniform' and their working
environment can all help to answer the questions 'Will I like it and
will I fit in?'.

At the end of the day, having worked out your style of dress and
behaviour, if there are occasional problems involving other people
and their acceptance of you, don't fall into the trap of thinking it is
all your fault.

> Women must stop feeling guilty and assuming that the problem is in
> themselves. . . If a man cannot cope with a woman being feminine,
> professional *and* highly skilled then perhaps he needs to ask himself
> a few questions.
>
> (Marilyn Davidson)

The question of what lies ahead for highly qualified women at work is one in which researchers are increasingly interested. In addition to the Manchester team already mentioned, the Institute of Employment Research (Warwick) and the Institute of Manpower Studies (Sussex) have produced a fund of knowledge and observations which are well worth reading.

## Further reading

Alston, A and Miller R (1987), *Equal Opportunities: A Careers Guide for Women and Men*, Harmondsworth, Penguin.

Bardwick, J (1986), *The Plateauing Trap*, New York, Bantam Books.

Bates, M and Kiersey, D (1984), *Please Understand Me*, California, Prometheus Nemesis.

Beck, J and Steel, M (1989), *Beyond the Great Divide: Introducing Equality into the Company*, London, Pitman.

Cohen, L (1985), *Women's Organisations in Great Britain*, London, Women's National Commission.

Cooper, C and Davidson, M (1982), *High Pressure: Working Lives of Women Managers*, London, Fontana.

Coyle, A and Skinner, J (1988), *Women and Work*, Basingstoke, Macmillan.

Davidson, M (1985), *Reach for the Top*, London, Piatkus.

Elias, P and Main, B (1982), *Women's Working Lives: Evidence from the National Training Survey*, University of Warwick, Institute for Employment Research.

Fritchie, R *et al.* (1983), *Women, Work and Training*, Sheffield, Manpower Services Commission (1986 supplement by Kay Smith Associates includes a Network list).

Hansard Society Commission (1990), *Women at the Top*, London, The Hansard Society for Parliamentary Government.

Hennig, M and Jardim, A (1976), *The Managerial Woman*, London, Marion Boyars.

Hunt, A, ed (1988), *Women and Paid Work*, Warwick Studies in Employment, Basingstoke, Macmillan.

Institute for Employment Research (1988), *Review of the Economy and Employment: Occupational Update*, University of Warwick.

Jones, B (1982), *Getting Ahead*, London, Ebury Press.

Josefowitz, N (1986), *Paths to Power*, London, Columbus Books.

Josefowitz, N (1987), *People Management*, London, Columbus Books.

Josefowitz, N (1988), *Fitting In*, Massachusetts, Addison-Wesley.

Kanter, R M (1977), *Men and Women of the Corporation*, New York, Basic Books.

La Rouche, J (1985) *Strategies for Women at Work*, London, Unwin Paperbacks.

Marshall, J (1984), *Women Managers: Travellers in a Male World*, Chichester, John Wiley.

Martin, J and Roberts, C (1984), *Women and Employment: A Lifetime Perspective*, London, HMSO.

Read, S (1982), *Sexual Harassment at Work*, Feltham, Hamlyn.

Roberts, S *et al.* (1981), *Positive Action for Women*, London, NCCL.

Scase, R and Goffee, R (1989), *Reluctant Managers: Their Work and Lifestyles*, London, Unwin Hyman.

Sedley, A and Benn, M (1982), *Sexual Harassment at Work*, London, NCCL.

Stamp, P and Roberts, S (1986), *Positive Action for Women at Work*, London, NCCL.

United Kingdom Inter-Professional Group (1990), *Women in the Professions*, London, Law Society.

Women in Management (1984), *Fact Sheets on Career Building*, Croydon.

See also: *Women and Training News*, published quarterly; *Graduate Working Women Casebook*, annual, Cambridge, Hobsons Publishing; and numerous network newsletters.

## Different ways to work

If you are a young jobhunter you should be aware of the various flexible working arrangements that exist, and the thinking behind them. Unlike the older graduate jobhunter, career changer or returner, however, it is less likely that you will be able to take advantage of them immediately. As it is quite possible that your view of a particular job or employer might be affected by such schemes, this section provides some background information for you. Consider the following passages from *Managing or Removing the Career Break* (MSC).

The rise of the Women's Movement, which brought about legislation on equal pay and opportunity and equality of education, has considerably changed the expectations of both women and men. Women have come to expect a continuation of their own life after children with the option of a job of equal status to men, whereas men are now wanting to be more involved in their children's lives in a meaningful way. To enable these changes to happen the fixed 40-hour working week must come to be seen as simply one variant among many possible arrangements, and not the norm against which all others are judged. This will demand a positive and innovative approach to working arrangements, a rethinking of conventional categories of work and a rigorous questioning of orthodoxies which on both economic and social evidence may no longer be serving us well.

More recently, The White Paper 'Employment for the 1990s' stated:

> The number of women in the labour force will increase. Two thirds of labour force growth between 1983 and 1987 was made up of married women, and by 1995 the projected increase in the size of the female labour force is some three quarters of a million, over 80 per cent of the total. Employers must recognise that women can no longer be treated as second class workers. They will need women employees, and must recognise their career ambitions and domestic responsibilities. This will involve broadening company training policies, much more flexibility of work and hours, and job sharing, to facilitate the employment of women with families and help adapt to their needs.

The Institute for Employment Research has argued:

> Over 90 per cent of individuals become parents at some stage in their lives. Policy measures. . .which promote flexible working arrangements for both women and *men* such as they constitute a normal phase of the life-cycle mix of paid and unpaid work would, over time, have a positive influence upon personal, interpersonal and institutional gender relationships.

Without such a central approach flexibility can become a dangerous word, disguising exploitation, for example.

Such provisos notwithstanding, the following are some of the most common ways in which flexibility has been introduced.

## *Jobsharing*

This is usually a working arrangement in which two people share the duties of one post, with pay, holidays and so on divided on a pro rata basis. It has been developed mainly by professional workers who have found that traditional part-time work (see page 86) is unsatisfactory – insecure, underpaid and low status. In fact, most jobs can be shared if the will exists, if ingenuity is applied, and if the potential jobsharers present a carefully argued case to potential employers, emphasising the positive advantages of such an arrangement. Such advantages include continuity, covering for holidays, double brainpower. Examples of job shares are:

| | |
|---|---|
| Solicitor | Careers officer |
| General practitioner | Social worker |
| Librarian | Publisher |
| Town planner | Training officer |
| Lecturer | Personnel officer |

Community worker                    Television producer
Researcher                          Nurse

New Ways to Work (see address on page 113) provides comprehensive advice on jobsharing and can put you in touch with projects,
jobsharing registers, and groups promoting this working method in
specific career areas. Here is how one advocate at the Hackney
Jobshare Project describes the advantages:

> Jobsharing looks at employment in a way that relates to the whole
> life, not just to work. It depends on a rethinking of the nature of work
> and its relation to time – not only daily, weekly and yearly but
> throughout the individual's lifespan. For many people it provides a
> means to achieve their personal fantasies and to live the life that they
> truly choose.
>
> Legislation on equal rights is based on the assumption that women
> only want to become full-time workers, and that by making women
> equivalent to men, equality is achieved. This does not take into
> account the fact that, for those with children, both women's and
> men's roles at work are intrinsically linked to their roles within the
> family. Perhaps the effect on the structure of the family is the most
> radical aspect of jobsharing. By allowing women and men to both
> work part-time and thus share childcare and domestic tasks, it can
> bring about a natural equality and a revolutionary new role model for
> the children. It improves the quality of life for women and men by
> allowing both to be active parents, and independent individuals in
> their own right.

## Sabbaticals/study leave

Sabbatical leave for a term, or a year, is one of the most envied
aspects of academic life. A period of refreshment, reflection and
research, preferably in an entirely different environment, can be
invigorating. It has been argued that without a concentrated period
of this type academics cannot keep up-to-date with their subject and
contribute to its body of research. Several female academics have
not only written research papers and books during this time but
have produced babies too!

As with jobsharing, if the will and ingenuity are there sabbaticals
can be introduced in other work areas too: academic-related jobs in
higher education, school teaching, local government, the medical
profession. Such schemes are common in many other countries,
why not the UK?

In-service training/secondment can be a form of sabbatical leave.
It may be hard work but at least the environment is different. Your
employer may decide that staff should have certain professional
qualifications, take a higher degree or exchange with someone in a
different environment (school/industry, for example) on full pay.

Sometimes you can be the initiator. Positive action programmes might be a help here. Many employers are either appointing equal opportunities officers or are anxious to be seen to be introducing career development programmes for all their staff. If an employer does not mention the opportunity for postgraduate study in a graduate recruitment brochure you could ask at an interview, 'I'm very keen to get on and I was wondering whether you ever send your marketing trainees on that specialist course at Polytechnic X?'

## Voluntary work

Unpaid work may lack the status of paid work in our society but in many ways it is every bit as vital to the economy. Where would our education, social services and health systems be without the contribution of numerous voluntary workers? The image of the lady of the manor moving among the poor dispensing charity has been hard to eradicate, and in some areas and in some charitable organisations perhaps a few of those attitudes on both 'sides' persist. However, organisations such as Community Service Volunteers have done much to dispense with these images, having accepted hundreds of volunteers from every imaginable background and all ages to work on a wide range of projects throughout the country. The skills used, acquired and developed in voluntary or paid work are usually equally valuable but are rarely equally valued. This is ironical. Voluntary work often provides the means of gaining that *previous relevant experience* so often mentioned in advertisements or course requirements, and provides a way of finding out about a work area before making a change in direction, or returning to paid work perhaps. Voluntary work can therefore be of great value to you and can involve as much commitment and responsibility as paid work.

## Flexitime

This is a very common working arrangement, often introduced in order to cope with travelling conditions as well as to provide staff coverage for longer periods. Schemes vary but typically the employer declares a 'core time' say 10 am to 3 pm when all staff must be present, with the other contractual hours to be worked in accordance with individual work needs and personal preferences.

## Part-time

Women working part time now account for almost half of all female employees (see Domestic Issues, page 93). This arrangement is a combination of necessity and choice. There is every sign that the trend towards an earlier return to work after having children, and a general increase in part-time work, will continue. Part-time work is often linked with skills-downgrading and lacks the security and status of full-time employment. Skills-downgrading means that a teacher might leave her job after five years' service and return to the labour market part time some years later as a secretary; meanwhile the qualified secretary might return as a filing clerk, and so on. One does not often hear examples of part-time workers returning to a higher-status occupation. The Institute of Employment Research at the University of Warwick has produced several fascinating studies of this topic.

## Home-based work

Computer programming is the professional job which is currently undertaken at home by considerable numbers of (mainly female) workers. Computer manufacturers such as STC-ICL, and the consultancy F International, are renowned for this working arrangement. It is especially suited to child-rearing but need not be exclusively so. Consultancy (tax, accountancy, careers as well as computing) and writing of all kinds obviously lend themselves to this arrangement. Of course, you can also be a self-employed freelance worker and be based at home too. The important characteristic of the schemes mentioned is that the workers have regular contracts of employment. It is likely that improved technology will mean that home-based work will increase in future and if, for example, such a work style became compulsory for groups of staff now working in office teams, there may well be some resistance given the various social needs which work also meets.

## Self-employment

In recent years there has been much government and individual interest in the option of self-employment. Such a choice might be a statement of individual philosophy and/or inspiration, a flight from the rat race and working hard for someone else's benefit rather than one's own and – rather more frequently in times of recession – the last hope of retrieving something for oneself from an increasingly difficult situation.

Women have contributed to the growth of many businesses over the centuries, occasionally for themselves but more often through a wide range of usually unpaid and hidden ways in their fathers' and/ or husband's enterprises; the butcher, baker and candlestick maker all received such support. More recently, and with the extension of franchises too, the balance is changing. According to figures released by the Training Agency in 1990, the number of people estimated to be self-employed in December 1989 was 3.252 million. Between December 1988 and December 1989, the number of self-employed grew by 198,000; 161,000 of these were men and 37,000 were women. The increase for both men and women was in full-time self-employment. Of course, not all new businesses succeed but many do and there has been considerable publicity about the many women who have become successful entrepreneurs in fields as varied as tax consultancy, software packaging, sports coaching, catering, photography and journalism.

Self-employment is one of the best-documented fields and large amounts of free literature as well as advice are available from the agencies listed in some of the references given below.

## Further reading

Alston, A and Miller, R (1989), *Hours to Suit*, London, Rosters.

Association of Graduate Careers Advisory Services Sex Equality Sub-Committee (1989), *Jobsharing*, AGCAS.

Boehm, K (1990), *The Careers Book 1991: Be Your Own Boss*, London, Macmillan.

Brady, L and Oppenheimer, S (1982), 'Job-sharing – a Discussion Paper', in *Managing or Removing the Career Break*, Sheffield, Manpower Services Commission.

Chapman, J (1989), *Women Working It Out*, Sheffield, Careers and Occupational Information Centre.

Elias, P and Main, B (1982), *Women's Working Lives: Evidence from the National Training Survey*, University of Warwick, Institute for Employment Research.

Equal Opportunities Commission (1985), *Code of Practice*, Manchester. Numerous other free booklets are available on request.

Everywoman (1990), *Directory of Women's Co-operatives and Other Enterprises: Women Mean Business*, London.

Fowler, D (1988), *The Women's Guide to Starting Your Own Business*, Grapevine.

Goffee, R and Scase, R (1985), *Women in Charge*, London, George Allen & Unwin.

Golzen, G (annual), *Working for Yourself – the Daily Telegraph Guide to Self-employment*, London, Kogan Page. There are many other relevant titles published by Kogan Page.

Humphries, J (1986), *Part-Time Work*, 2nd edn, London, Kogan Page.

Hunt, A, ed (1988), *Women and Paid Work*, Warwick Studies in Employment, Basingstoke, Macmillan.

Kirkman, W and Ward, A (1990), *Small Businesses: Theirs or Yours?* Manchester, Association of Graduate Careers Advisory Services.

Martin, J and Roberts, C (1984), *Women and Employment: A Lifetime Perspective*, London, HMSO.

New Ways to Work, numerous leaflets available on request (see address on page 113).

Syrett, M (1985), *Goodbye 9 - 5*, London, New Opportunity Press.

Walton, P (1990), *Job Sharing: A Practical Guide for Women*, London, Kogan Page.

## Career breaks

Women play an increasingly important role in the total professional and managerial workforce and the extension of graduate entry schemes in many areas seems likely to continue. Employers will want to retain this important sector of their skilled staff rather than lose their own considerable investment in training and valuable expertise, contacts and suchlike. How might they achieve this?

As we saw in Different Ways to Work on page 83, although there is a recognition of an employee's family commitments, a willingness to consider periods of part-time work or other flexible arrangements, it remains very difficult for a woman to continue working full time when she has young children. Although it is no longer expected that a woman should give up her job on marriage or parenthood, lack of facilities for appropriate child-care, including employer crèches, cause problems. The 1990 March Budget included a tax concession for workplace nurseries. This led to a flurry of publicity and press comment about such facilities which are extremely rare. Some employers feel that the provision of nurseries is the answer to their retention problems, while others, aware of the realities of commuting for adults let alone accompanied by toddler(s) and pushchair, are less convinced. Organisations such as Childcare Vouchers are approaching the problem from a wider and more varied standpoint. Britain lags behind its European partners with, for example, only 2 per cent of under two-year-olds in state controlled and funded day care whereas such provision is available to 25 per cent of French, 44 per cent of Danish and 30 per cent of West Germans of the same age group.

The issue of appropriate and widely available child-care remains central to the question of career breaks for women with children. There is also an underlying and erroneous assumption that care is no longer needed once a child starts school. Be this as it may, an increasing number of employers are introducing formal career breaks and formal returner schemes which have received considerable publicity in recent years. What are these schemes and how might they affect you?

'Career break' covers several arrangements:

—extended maternity leave, any period beyond the statutory allowance
—guaranteed return to work after several years' absence on certain conditions, eg maintaining professional links with the employer
—guaranteed return to work on a part-time or jobsharing basis
—re-recruitment after absence, depending on the availability of a suitable vacancy.

Some employers offer career breaks to all their staff. Others concentrate on managers. Of course, if you possess the skills and attributes which your employer needs you are in a stronger bargaining position. Such bargaining might be needed for secondment or study leave but is most commonly needed for motherhood. (Imagine if fatherhood had to be regarded in this way.) At a Manpower Services Commission (now the Training Agency) conference in 1981 the phrase 'maternal brain drain' was coined. As with other brain drains attempts to counter this one are spasmodic and meet with varied success.

At first sight career break schemes seem marvellous. Those agonising decisions about when/if to start a family and when/if to re-enter the labour market are resolved. The facts are less cheerful. Thus, while it is thought politic to be seen to be concerned about the retention of highly qualified women, relatively few employers have introduced full-scale schemes, preferring to deal with individual cases as they arise and being sensitive to precedents.

In a research report published by the Institute of Manpower Studies in 1985 (*Women, Career Breaks and Re-entry*) several factors emerged as barriers to the introduction of a scheme:

—female wastage suits some organisations as this sustains good promotion prospects for men (yes, it was recognised that women were proportionately better than men, hence the relief at their departure)
—failure to cost the benefits of retainer schemes
—reactive rather than proactive attitude among senior management
—unwillingness to adopt flexibility in any aspect of an organisation
—resistance to women in management (you should be aware

of this resistance which is disguised with varying degrees of subtlety, 'Male managers as husbands and fathers frequently have deeply ambivalent attitudes towards encouraging women to combine motherhood with work').

Thus, if a scheme exists it is probably as a result of considerable negotiation and controversy.

Employers rarely mention career break schemes in their recruitment literature but this may change when the link between such schemes and recruitment as well as retention is shown. Although some schemes have received considerable general press publicity, do not assume that just because a large organisation has obtained beneficial publicity about how it has retained high flying managers this will affect how your first male boss treats you, perhaps his first woman graduate trainee! Another pitfall of this publicity is that the impression can be given that dozens of women are involved when it may only be a handful so far. Bearing in mind that each scheme is different and that circumstances can change rapidly, here are some examples of employers offering career breaks:

National Health Service (retainer schemes for doctors and dentists)
Civil Service
Most large firms of chartered accountants
Most large banks
Local government (eg special schemes for social workers and housing managers)
The legal profession
An increasing number of industrial organisations.

If you are interested in other work areas it is well worth enquiring about career break arrangements. As the effects of demographic changes are felt, more and more employers will want not only to attract but also to retain their staff – that means you too.

When discussing career breaks there is a danger of making assumptions that these are synonymous with parenthood.

We sometimes talk as though it is only women with children who have breaks from employment. This is, of course, not true. Many employees have breaks of one kind or another from their normal job. Some are transferred elsewhere for a period either to deal with a crisis or to give them wider experience. Others may be sent away for training or education – the one year at a management training centre for the high flyer. Some leave one employer to go off to another organisation, and may later return. In some industries such as the computer industry, it is seen as quite reasonable to do this. Some in the past went on military service and others now are made redundant in their field at an early age. All these people have needed to be reintegrated to some extent when they returned to work. None of these breaks is seen as an insuperable obstacle, and many are seen as positive. Employees are seen as coming back with new knowledge, confidence, experience.

Margery Povall, *Managing or Removing the Career Break*

It is also unfair to deduce that all career break schemes exclude men. The very fact that such an assumption is made indicates how deep-rooted some attitudes are. In recent years there has been some debate about 'parenthood' or 'nominated carer' leave being more appropriate wording, given the changing nature of family and social relationships.

## Engineering: a special case

The engineering profession is one which has been forced to look at career breaks as a way of resolving the wider issue of recruitment and retention. The proportion of women on engineering and technology courses in higher education has increased but not to the extent that many argue the country needs. During the 1980s there were several campaigns to encourage women to consider careers in science, technology and engineering and to ensure that they had studied the necessary subjects in school to enable them to make such a choice. These campaigns included Women into Science and Engineering (WISE), launched jointly with the Equal Opportunities Commission in 1984, and Industry Year in 1986. Early in 1990 Women into Information Technology was formed, one in a long line of 'Women into . . .' campaigns, all of which are helpful in raising the profile of work areas previously assumed to be male preserves. Radio and television programmes, together with newspaper and magazine articles, have complemented such efforts so that today's schoolgirls and first-time jobhunters have far more role models to consider than their mothers had. The Engineering Council has supported all these developments and since 1985 has campaigned for organisations employing chartered and technician engineers to review their policies towards career breaks as part of their overall approach to continuing education and training for employees. It was argued that 'those organisations that develop positive policies towards career breaks stand to attract more able women who will wish to combine a career in engineering with having a family'. In its survey of women members, *Career Breaks for Women Chartered and Technician Engineers*, the Institution of Electrical Engineers found considerable interest in career breaks and it concluded that students will be attracted to employers who demonstrate a flexible approach, and that girls at school might be more inclined to choose an engineering career if they knew that this was the case. Various schemes have been introduced to aid the returning engineer. For example, in September 1990 Women into Industry launched pilot courses leading to an MSc in Manufacturing Management at the Cranfield Institute of Technology and the University of Bradford. These courses are for women returners who already have first degrees in engineering, science or technology, ideally with some industrial experience, who wish to refresh and develop their ideas further.

## Further reading

Alston, A and Miller, R (1987), *Equal Opportunities: A Careers Guide for Women and Men*, Harmondsworth, Penguin (includes a section on career breaks after each entry).

Engineering Council (1985), *Career Breaks for Women Chartered and Technician Engineers*, London.

Engineering Council (1989), *Engineering Equals*, London.

Engineering Council (1990), *Women into Science and Engineering: Awards, Courses, Visits*, London.

Hirsh, W *et al.* (1985), *Women, Career Breaks and Re-Entry*, Brighton, Institute of Manpower Studies.

Metcalf, H (1990), *Under-Utilisation of Women in the Labour Market*, Brighton, Institute of Manpower Studies.

Moloney, K (1985), *Developing Your Womanpower*, London, Industrial Society.

Povall, M and Hastings, J (1981), *Managing or Removing the Career Break*, Sheffield, Manpower Services Commission.

Rajan, A (1989), *Good Practices in the Employment of Women Returners*, Brighton, Institute of Manpower Services.

## Domestic issues

The dawn of the 1990s saw an upsurge of interest in a debate on life-style and work-style issues not only for individual women and men but for employing organisations. For a range of circumstantial reasons, such as demographic trends, rather than from any commitment to equal opportunities as such it has become far more common for employers to consider family issues and for the Government and public figures to comment upon them. You will need to look behind the 'hype' and discover the facts. Stating 'we are (or strive to be) an equal opportunities employer' is not enough. What is being done to enable women and men of all social and ethnic back-grounds and circumstances to achieve their full potential? What might they offer *you*?

As the population is ageing, you also need to consider a current or future role as a carer. Thus domestic issues/family responsibilities are likely to include parental as well as child-care.

Despite this broader debate the possibility of marriage and mother-hood affects the way in which many employers regard applications from women and the way in which women often plan their careers. Brenda Jones states: 'I've yet to be on a campus where women weren't worrying about some aspect of combining marriage, children and a career – and I've yet to find one where men were worrying about the same thing.'

Test-tube babies notwithstanding, it remains a fact that pregnancy and childbirth are exclusively female activities and it is this fact that is used to discriminate against women. Often this discrimination is unfair. Not all woman will be able or anxious to have children. Not all women will want to leave the labour market for very long after childbirth, and a higher proportion of women are returning to work before their youngest child starts primary school. Some of the impli-cations of this are discussed in a research report (Martin and Roberts, 1984) which shows:

> . . .the choices women . . . are making about combining work and home and the factors which influence these choices. Most women are happy about their balance of home and work, and often part-time employment has been a crucial way in which they have achieved this. For the minority of women who choose or need to effect a different balance the position is less clear cut. Some, like lone parents . . . may be particularly disadvantaged by having to combine domestic and paid work without a partner. Other women may make a different choice, emphasising paid work; if they are highly qualified and work full time in higher level jobs they are most likely of all women to work on comparable terms with men. What is clear is that most women, unlike most men, both have the choice and often still have to choose.

Whether or not you feel this is fair, or whether it affects you person-ally at any stage in your life, you will be affected at least marginally through your colleagues, friends and family.

Society continues to provide women with a thoroughly respectable alternative to paid work outside the home, ie to undertake unpaid work within the home! Some men are subconsciously, if not openly, jealous of this choice, the freedom it implies and the honourable escape from the rat race it represents. A few men by choice and some by force of circumstance have exchanged the main bread-winning role with their partner but this remains a rare arrangement.

It is implicit that children are the joint responsibility of parents. It is less common to regard them as an equal responsibility. It would be unfair to enthusiastic fathers, especially single parents, to assume that women are automatically better at caring for children. Such a monopolistic attitude on the part of women can be as unfair as men who say women can't manage.

(Virginia Novarra)

Many women feel very uneasy about any such threat to one of their few areas of power and influence, the home.

Of course, domesticity and particularly motherhood bestow a status which can be misleading, especially to the young, and is invariably short-lived. Think about the glamorous image of domesticity projected by many advertisements. Then think about the last time you saw a parent struggling with a baby in a pushchair, reluctant toddler in tow, clutching shopping bags and trying to get on a bus or train.

It seems particularly cruel of society to encourage young women to give up paid employment when their children are small and then, instead of rewarding them for this allegedly socially beneficial sacrifice, to penalise them for the rest of their working lives.

(Virginia Novarra)

Not so long ago there was a stigma attached to a woman who worked outside the home as this was seen as a sign that her husband could not keep her. Being able to say, 'I'm a housewife' was a statement of one's respectable and respected social status. Times have changed and the term 'housewife' or 'homemaker' is often a low status role, hence that apologist phrase 'I'm only a housewife'. For a variety of complex reasons well documented elsewhere, women tend to

undervalue their role as housewives ... Being a housewife is a demanding and important job whether or not you like it or feel you are good at it. Unlike most other jobs, it's one without initial training, with a standard rate of payment, without a formal contract governing hours and conditions of service, and without any career prospects.

(D Perry)

Of course, some women are quite happy being housewives. This book is certainly not criticising those who have made, and have been able to make, such a choice. However, it is relatively common for women who have made being a housewife their initial career to want a change later on, when children leave home, when death/divorce/partner's redundancy forces a re-think, for instance.

Another point which is rarely mentioned concerns family planning. No method of birth control is perfect and the assumption that the pill and coil have removed all risks of unwanted pregnancy is a cruel one. No matter how much you may think April 19XX would be a good time to have a baby, things may not work out that way. So, there are still considerable numbers of women facing unplanned pregnancies who have taken every reasonable precaution, and another group who desperately want to conceive but do not do so. As yet there is no equality in biology!

Proportionately more graduates have long-term career aspirations. It is likely that any future partner will have a similar educational and occupational background to your own. It is quite likely that you will become a dual-career couple, each of you respecting the other's job aspirations and agreeing the implicit give and take involved. This can put a strain on a relationship. The strain can occur at the initial jobhunting stage. Where will you look? Will your partner be willing to fit in if you get a job first? Are you willing to be separated for a time for a training course or a secondment, for example? What happens if you become what is termed the career leader, ie if you do better and earn more? How might you cope with the consequent jealousy? These are extremely difficult questions. The fact that there are no easy answers accounts for the incidence of later marriage and certainly later maternity of highly qualified women, some divorce or separation, and in some cases a decision to remain single. All this points to the rather unromantic notion that it is sensible to choose like-minded partners and then to plan your respective careers and private lives as much as possible. Such an approach may be dismissed as calculating as well as unromantic. Try not to be put off by it: such forward thinking will pay off for both of you. An increasing number of couples are trying to plan in this way to the extent that some long-held assumptions are no longer appropriate. Your partner's job buys freedom of a sort because fewer people are willing to uproot when a career move of maybe only two years' duration is involved, more are prepared to commute, and some are prepared to pass up a promotion in order to support a partner's career demands or maintain an aspect of their personal life which they value. Such changes in attitudes are causing many organisations to review their promotion policies, for example.

Another reason to discuss immediate and longer-term plans with your partner is to avoid 'role overload', ie you working a 40-hour week, bringing work home, doing all the domestic chores plus a lot of business entertaining, and maybe looking after your children's social and other interests too! Negotiating task-sharing with your partner is crucial, and you may be willing and able to buy in some extra help, too. Of course, if you are a single person household you will carry this additional burden alone and many senior women managers have commented that what they really need is a traditional housewife to support their domestic role! It has been said that the campaign for equal opportunities has meant that women won the right to be eternally exhausted. If not eternally exhausted, women seem eternally guilty:

> If I'm in the office
> I wish I were home
> With the children
> If I'm home with the children
> I know I should be
> In the office
> I always should be
> Wherever
> I'm not!

(N. Josefowitz)

One thing seems certain in your future: you will have to work out a balance between your domestic and your other roles. Your balance may be different from that of your friends, colleagues or neighbours, but you will need to find it. Such a balance is likely to change during your life as circumstances alter, and perhaps your views and priorities change. It is salutory to bear in mind that research on the health of women and men shows that greater equality in life-style may mean greater equality in death-style. Time spent considering your personal priorities, devising means to manage stress, for example, is always time well spent.

## Further reading

Davidson, M (1985), *Reach for the Top*, London, Piatkus.

Dowling, C (1981), *The Cinderella Complex – Women's Hidden Fear of Independence*, London, Fontana.

Fogarty, M P *et al.* (1971), *Sex, Career and Family*, London, Allen & Unwin.

Fogarty, M *et al.* (1981), *Women and Top Jobs 1968–1979*, London, Heinemann.

Foster, J (1988), 'Balancing Work and the Family: Divided Loyalties or Constructive Partnership', *Personnel Management*.

Hansard Society Commission (1990), *Women at the Top*, London, Hansard Society.

Jones, B (1982), *Cosmopolitan Guide to Getting Ahead*, London, Ebury Press.

Martin, J and Roberts, C (1984), *Women and Employment: A Lifetime Perspective*, London, HMSO.

Moss, P and Fonda, N, eds (1980), *Work and the Family*, London, Temple Smith.

Novarra, V (1980), *Women's Work, Men's Work*, London, Marion Boyars.

Oakley, A (1974), *Housewife*, Harmondsworth, Pelican.

Oakley, A (1981), *Subject Women*, Oxford, Martin Robertson.

Opportunities for Women (1990), *Carers at Work*, London, OFW.

Perry, D *et al.* (1983), *What Else Can A Housewife Do?* Sheffield, MSC/COIC.

Radcliffe Richards, J (1980), *The Sceptical Feminist*, London, Routledge & Kegan Paul.

Rapoport, R and R (1971), *Dual Career Families*, Harmondsworth, Pelican.

Scase, R and Goffee, R (1989), *Reluctant Managers: Their Work and Lifestyles*, London, Unwin Hyman.

Sex Equality Sub-Committee (1990), *Lifestyle/Workstyle: Getting It Right*, AGCAS.

Sharpe, S (1986), *Double Identity: The Lives of Working Mothers*, Harmondsworth, Pelican.

# Chapter 7

# Mature Students, Returners and Career Changers

If you are not a typical 21-year-old graduate you may have felt excluded from some of the advice and comments offered so far. Much of the general information is relevant to all jobhunters but there are some additional points which are particularly relevant to you.

You may have noticed already that there are many publications aimed at you and your concerns. A selection of these is listed in the further reading list on page 103 and you can find many of this chapter's themes elaborated elsewhere if you wish. The current emphasis on training and retraining, personal and career development, increased leisure time, redundancy and early retirement, demographic trends (an ageing population), expansion of adult and continuing education facilities, means that there are likely to be even more schemes and literature targeted at you in the 1990s.

Self-help is a feature of the late twentieth century so it is ultimately up to you to decide what, if any, action you want to take as a result of your investigations. Whether you want to retrain after a period away from education and employment, or change the course of your career completely, or perhaps set up in business on your own, you will need plenty of guts and determination.

*Personal transferable skills* is a career phrase which is popular at the moment and it is especially relevant to the older jobhunter. As you saw in Chapter 4, these are skills which have been obtained in one context which are relevant elsewhere. Words such as *plan*, *supervise*, *persuade*, *negotiate*, *budget*, *motivate*, *responsibility*, *decision*, *conciliate*, *co-operation*, *conflicting demands*, *time management*, can be used to describe domestic activities or experience in voluntary work as well as tasks undertaken in the factory, office, laboratory or other working environment. Start making your own list. Promise yourself that you will be positive. Never use 'I'm too old' or 'No one will take a risk on me' or 'I've never done anything' as an excuse or an explanation or an expectation. Get in there and have a go. Prove the sceptics wrong!

An exhortation to be positive is not to deny that you must be even more determined to persevere, to be original and ingenious in your job search, and that you should never be too proud to seek advice, even from a younger person.

You have numerous counter-arguments in favour of employing older women should you be faced by discriminatory questions in a job interview. Women live approximately seven years longer than men. Older candidates have usually had their families, and the demands of school examinations can mean that career moves for either parent can be less frequent for some years. Many older women experience a period of renewed activity and a positive wish to experience new things which mean they have a great deal to offer employers at this stage. It is also true that nowadays it is very rare for someone to enter a first job with a realistic chance of remaining with that first employer throughout his or her working life. Changes of job specialism, retraining associated with the introduction of new technology, for example, possible periods of unemployment too, have become common experiences for men as well as women. As we saw in Chapter 6, men as well as women have 'breaks' of one sort and another. What matters in jobhunting contexts is what experience was gained and how that experience is projected.

In a survey conducted in 1988 employers were asked 'what do you regard as the advantages of employing mature graduates?' Here are some of the advantages:

| | |
|---|---|
| above average performance | realism |
| better at handling clients | judgement |
| more pragmatic | more worldly |
| need less supervision | genuine commitment |
| well rounded | determined |
| highly developed personal skills | less inclined to pursue tangential matters |

Singing the praises of the mature jobhunter in this way may boost the ego but you should also bear in mind that many employers remain locked in stereotyped assumptions about mature applicants and you may well encounter unreasonably ageist attitudes.

What might that mean for you? If you see age limits in advertisements but feel you have most of the other requirements specified, try sending a brief covering letter with your application form or CV stating that you are confident you can do the job, that you have plenty to offer, and that you trust you would not be eliminated on age grounds alone. If you have also highlighted ways in which your previous experience is relevant to the job as described you could well be considered. Don't necesarily take 'no' for an answer.

You might have read so far and are muttering, 'That's all very well but. . .'. The 'yes but' syndrome in delayed decision-making is well documented. It goes hand in hand with 'it will be possible when . . . the children are older/we have more money/the winter's over. . .', and similar excuses which cover human apprehension about change and decisions and possibly awkward situations. Hiding behind such phrases can be a symptom of loss of confidence, too. Again, this is a well-documented phenomenon so don't feel you are alone. This loss of confidence can follow job loss, a series of rejections in the job market or in personal life, as well as being a common side-effect of years outside the job market. It can be very hard to boost confidence, especially if family and so-called friends are undermining you or making you feel guilty. Job advertisements can cause a crisis of confidence, too. They invariably require 'previous relevant experience', don't they? Almost invariably, many potential candidates – including you perhaps – are put off. Had you ever considered that you might be too modest, that there was no reason at all to be put off? In many cases, having more than half the skills and attributes mentioned in a job description or further particulars could be sufficient to be considered as a serious candidate. Employers often use a job description to remind themselves of the 'ideal' candidate, the person who could miraculously perform all those tasks that somehow all previous incumbents of the position had failed to do. There is no reason to suppose that their luck will turn this time, that Superperson will appear. Yes, there is hope for *you*.

If you are currently considering a return to study and/or employment you will stand a better chance of making a decision which is right for *you* if you spend time researching options and possible outcomes *before* you commit yourself. Many mature graduates were bitten by the education bug as a result of registering for a single course at their local further education college. 'Return to Learn', 'Wider Opportunities for Women' and many other short courses are now available but on a rather spasmodic basis. Check with your local education authority and higher education institutions, or refer to the directories produced for the Women Returners' Network and the Educational Counselling and Credit Transfer Information Service (ECCTIS). Most adult and extra-mural/open studies courses now offer some options which are directed specifically at women. The Open University continues to offer seemingly endless scope for self-fulfilment and change. Open Tech, the University of the Third Age and other institutions aimed at the non-traditional student market look set to expand. There is something to suit every taste and educational ability.

Some higher education institutions, the University of Warwick and Coventry Polytechnic, for example, have a long tradition of access courses whereby students who have participated in special programmes at local further education colleges can be considered for entry to full- or part-time degree courses without the usual entry qualifications. In recent years other institutions have formulated wider access policies, in some cases more as a reaction to the likely effect of demographic changes than as a genuine concern about adult learners.

You should look behind some of the hype about courses. Always consult adult education advisory services, careers services, course tutors and others who can provide an objective assessment of the implications of further study. Be honest with yourself about your objectives. If you feel a degree will automatically open more career doors for you, check whether that expectation is correct as far as your chosen institution, course and personal circumstances are concerned. A vocational sandwich course may increase your chances. If you are enthusiastic about a particular subject and want to study it further for its own sake, fine. Thus, taking a philosophy degree won't necessarily improve employment prospects, but it might be enormously valuable in personal development terms.

Of course, no one can offer you guaranteed results, but you can give yourself the best possible chance of success in your terms if you research carefully *before* you begin a course. Once a student, it is advisable to consult your careers service early so that you can gather up-to-date information about job entry requirements and employer attitudes to older applicants, and participate in potentially useful events such as careers information fairs and employer visits.

Mature students have every reason to be optimistic. A survey by the Council for National Academic Awards (CNAA) found that 'non-traditional students perform better in their final degrees than those who enter higher education after A levels'. There are several reasons for this – high motivation and a determination to prove one-self being particularly common. The experience of mature students in higher education is well documented. Look through material in your local careers service or consult some of the listed books, together with the invaluable materials produced by the AGCAS Sub-Committee on the Employment and Training of the Older Graduate. These should convince you that most if not all of your apprehensions have been anticipated, that you are not alone.

Courses of various types undoubtedly provide a useful opportunity to assess your personal commitment and the practical consequences of a return to paid work or a change in direction. Change can lead to personal conflict too, sometimes a growing away from your partner, or family, or friends. Finding what is right for *you* at this stage in your life may prove risky. It may also turn out to be the best thing you ever did!

## Further reading

Alston, A and Miller R (1987), *Equal Opportunities: A Careers Guide for Women and Men*, Harmondsworth, Penguin.

Ball, B (1989), *Manage Your Own Career: A Self-Help Guide to Career Choice and Change*, London, Kogan Page.

Bardwick, J (1986), *The Plateauing Trap*, New York, Bantam Books.

Bayley, J (1990), *How to Get a Job After 45*, London, Kogan Page.

Bell, J and Roderick, G (1982), *Never Too Late to Learn*, London, Longman.

Bolles, R N (1990), *What Colour is Your Parachute?*, Berkeley, Ten Speed Press.

*British Qualifications*, annual, London, Kogan Page.

Dobbie, E (1982), *Returners*, London, National Advisory Centre on Women.

ECCTIS (1989), *Access to Higher Education Courses Directory*, London, CNAA.

Good, M and Pates, A (1989), *Second Chances*, Sheffield, Careers & Occupational Information Centre.

Graham, B (1989), *Older Graduates and Employment*, Manchester, Central Services Unit.

Hopson, B and Scally, M (1984), *Build Your Own Rainbow: A Workbook for Career and Life Management*, Leeds, Lifeskills Associates.

Jones, A *et al.* (1989), for AGCAS, *What Do Graduates Do?*, Cambridge, Hobsons Publishing.

Korving, M (1990), *Mature Student's Handbook*, London, Kogan Page.

Korving, M (1990), *Nursing as a Second Career*, London, Kogan Page.

Morphy, L (1986), *Career Change*, Cambridge, Hobsons Publishing.

Pearson, R *et al.* (1989), *How Many Graduates in the 21st Century?*, Brighton, Institute of Manpower Studies.

Reed, A (1989), *Returning to Work: A Practical Guide for Women*, London, Kogan Page.

Smith, M (1989), *The Best is Yet to Come*, Leeds, Lifeskills Associates.

Smith, M (1989), *Branching Out: A Workbook for Early Retirement*, Leeds, Lifeskills Associates.

Straw, J (1989), *Equal Opportunities*, London, Institute of Personnel Management.

Sub-Committee on the Employment and Training of the Older Graduate (1983), *Thinking About Higher Education*, Association of Graduate Careers Advisory Services.

Sub-Committee on the Employment and Training of the Older Graduate (1988), *Older Graduates' Career Resource Pack*, Association of Graduate Careers Advisory Services.

Sub-Committee on the Employment and Training of the Older Graduate (1988), *Survey of Employer Attitudes Towards the Recruitment and Employability of the Older Graduate*, Association of Graduate Careers Advisory Services.

Sub-Committee on the Employment and Training of the Older Graduate (1989), *Older Graduates and Employment*, Association of Graduate Careers Advisory Services.

Training Agency/Careers Occupational Information Centre (COIC) publications include February 1988, supplement on 'Age and Employment' in *Newscheck*, What Else Can . . . Do Series (Housewife, Teacher, Nurse, You), and 'Women Working It Out'.

Women Returners' Network (1990), *Returning to Work*, London, Kogan Page.

*Women and Training News*, quarterly, Women and Training Group.

Leaflets for mature students are published by the Committee of Vice Chancellors and Principals (CVCP), the Council for National Academic Awards and individual institutions.

Lists of courses and entry qualifications appear in several of the reference books. Hobsons Publishing launched the *Returners Magazine* in 1990.

The Open University publishes a series of leaflets aimed at the older, graduate jobhunter.

Television programmes occasionally feature career changers and women returners, eg Spring 1990, *Women Mean Business* for which there was an accompanying information booklet.

The Pepperell Unit of the Industrial Society has launched a series of 'Back to the Future' conferences and other events for women considering a return to work.

## Chapter 8
# Getting In and Getting On — Some Personal Experiences

The following case studies are all genuine although the names of individuals are different.

| | |
|---|---|
| *Mary* | Secretarial training and several years' work experience before having children. Occasional part-time work when children were young, then A level psychology and English via a local 'Access' scheme leading to a degree course in philosophy. Taught herself to program. After a year as an administrator for a national charity, obtained a research assistantship where academic ability plus the practical skills of typing and programming are crucial. |
| *Jean* | Left school at 16, worked in the retail industry for some years then felt that higher education would open up more possibilities. Took A levels at the local technical college through evening classes and registered for an Open University degree. After two years transferred, with OU credits, to her local polytechnic to study social administration. A long track record of voluntary work with young offenders meant that she was accepted on to a Certificate in Qualified Social Work (CQSW) course for the October after graduation. |
| *Debbie* | Took a modern languages degree immediately after leaving school. The idea of BBC studio management had appealed ever since a fourth form visit to her local radio station. In her first summer vacation she got a clerical job in the BBC and used that to find out as much as possible about the organisation, especially the technical specialist jobs within it. Repeated this in the second summer vacation. She was also involved with her campus radio station, and |

spent time in the audio-visual unit whenever possible, familiarising herself with a wide range of equipment. In her final year applied successfully for the BBC Studio Management Training Scheme.

*Jo*  Always wanted to get into journalism. She had edited the school magazine and had spent several weeks with her local newspaper on a work experience scheme. As soon a she began her politics degree course she signed up to help the team producing the student newspaper. Every vacation she worked voluntarily for a local newspaper. Despite an impressive track record of relevant experience, and lots of contacts, she failed to get one of the few places on a journalist training scheme. However, three months after graduation, a contact did remember her as a result of which another local newspaper wanting a general reporter asked her for interview. This meant starting at the bottom but. . .

*Sarah*  Half way through her classics course she decided that advertising was for her. None of the talk about long hours, constant pressure, numeracy, tough negotiations, effect on private life, could dissuade her. She followed up what few advertisements there were but made numerous speculative approaches too, one of which came off and she became a media buyer with a top agency.

*Sue*  Music and maths had been her joint passions for years. In her second year she decided that the actuarial profession was the one most likely to give her professional and academic satisfaction, with some flexibility too. While boyfriend Dave hunted for a funded postgraduate place in the United States, she found a consultant actuary firm which was willing to train her in the US with the possibility of a transfer back to the UK once the PhD was completed.

*Penny*  After a second year psychology project involving an attitude survey, she became interested in market research. Realising that few of the consultancies advertise and that those that do tend to start recruiting early, she planned her applications early and also wrote dozens of speculative letters. Dozens of rejection letters came, but so did a few invitations to interviews, one of which led to a job offer.

*Jackie*   During her sociology course she decided on a career in personnel/industrial relations. She decided to concentrate on manufacturing industry, ignoring comments about women entering predominantly male working environments. She got a vacation job in a large car company and found she enjoyed the atmosphere and could cope with the work, so decided to apply for a permanent job with them. Having observed her for eight weeks, the company was impressed and took her on.

*Beth*   Had always been good at physics and never had a second thought when offered a place on a degree course. Despite talk about shortage of physics teachers and the need for physicists in industry, in the middle of her final year she suddenly felt she had had enough of the subject. She decided that stockbroking would offer a complete contrast, applied to a large firm and was successful at her first attempt (extremely unusual).

*Ann*   A teenage marriage and three children in quick succession meant that further education was not feasible for some time. A deep interest in her own children's education, a short spell as teacher's helper, and involvement with Brownies, led to the decision to try to become a teacher. Having obtained additional O (including the compulsory maths and English language) and A levels she was accepted by her local university for a BEd course. Four years later all her perseverance paid off as not only did she obtain her degree but also obtained one of the few teaching posts that were advertised in her area.

| | |
|---|---|
| *Louise* | Despite a continued liking of English as a subject she decided to go for chartered accountancy. Having A level maths helped a lot but so did her active involvement in student societies, vacation work and general enthusiasm for professional training. She soon received several job offers. One of the factors which influenced her choice was the number of women staff and the attitude of staff at all levels to career breaks. |
| *Joy* | Having left school after A levels she spent some years jobhopping – book and record shops, general clerical jobs – and had two children. By the age of 25 she felt ready to appreciate higher education. Her partner fully supported the idea and determined to be an active parent. Not only did she cope with her history course but was an active member of several student societies and her local constituency party. Initially unable to achieve her goal of a management job locally, she was asked to help at her local further education college where she found she had a rare gift for teaching reluctant learners. |
| *Helen* | Unexpectedly pregnant during her second year, daughter born in the middle of the summer vacation. Numerous money problems especially as partner was on a small postgraduate grant. With the help of her student colleagues as well as her partner and his friends, and the support of her academic department, she managed to get a good degree and obtained a job teaching English as a foreign language. |
| *Pat* | Had never had a second thought about becoming a civil engineer. Decided to apply for jobs with large consultancy firms with the medium-term goal of overseas assignments. Having qualified in record time and already respected by her employers she achieved her ambition and was appointed project leader on a Middle East contract. |
| *Jane* | Having taken a business studies degree and taught in secondary schools for some years, |

decided a change of direction was needed. Made speculative approaches to industrial organisations, several of whom were interested which gave her the confidence to be selective. Eventually obtained a training officer job with a leading food manufacturer.

*Kate*    After a degree in dance and drama took a graduate personal assistant's course at her local technical college. Was the star student in her year. Obtained a job in her area health authority where she was quickly used in the personnel rather than the personal assistant role.

*Jess*    Wanted to continue her academic career in economics eventually but after a Master's degree decided to get some practical experience before her PhD. Received a lucrative offer from a management consultancy, with the possibility of a MBA at an American business school if all went well in the first two years.

*Rachel*    Despite her PhD in English prospects of obtaining a lecturer post seemed remote. She decided to obtain a mixture of work experience, hoping that a full-time position might materialise eventually. Her part-time jobs included A level tutoring, Open Studies course teaching, evening library assistant duties, and further education lecturing. She still keeps in touch with her former academic department in case the 'grapevine' receives news of any possible openings before they are advertised.

These case studies show that there are numerous ways of getting where you want to be, and that many jobs are open to graduates of any discipline.

## Further reading

*Graduate Working Women Casebook*, Cambridge, Hobsons Publishing, one of a series published annually.

*Women in Industry* (1981), Cambridge, CRAC/Hobsons Press.

*Women in Research in GEC* (1982), London, The General Electric Company plc.

Many of the books listed as further reading for other sections in this book also include case histories which are an excellent way of answering that important question, 'But what is it *really* like?' Recruitment brochures frequently include case histories too.

# Conclusion

The main conclusion that may be drawn from this book is that there *are* opportunities for *you*. You have to work hard to get them *but* help is at hand *and* you can often make your own luck.

To make the most of opportunities you need to be clear what you want, and why, where the vacancies are, and how to make an effective case for yourself. If this book has helped you in this search it has achieved its objective.

Obviously not everyone wants, or can, get to 'the top' – however that is defined. But everyone can get 'there'. We cannot do it alone. We need the encouragement and moral support of our partners, friends and colleagues, female and male alike. We need encouragement to discover who we are, what we want, and what we have to give. We need to be enabled to develop our full potential. We need to find a balance in our lives which suits *us* – not the statistical norm, not the neighbours, but us. Only then might it be said that we have got 'there'.

At no point in this book is there a claim to provide all the answers to all the imponderables in your life or that of anyone else. What it does claim to achieve is to make you think about yourself, about those close to you, about your preferences and priorities, and about what might await you in the world of work.

That first step in jobhunting can be crucial. I hope that this book will encourage you to stride out with confidence. Good luck!

# Useful Addresses

Depending on your particular interest, further information may be obtainable from one or several of the organisations listed below. Many of the publications included in the further reading lists contain yet more addresses.

*Association of Graduate Careers Advisory Services*
c/o Chris Philips
Honorary Secretary
Careers and Appointments Service
University of Manchester
Crawford House
Precinct Centre
Manchester M13 9QS

*Careers for Women*
4th Floor
2 Valentine Place
London SE1 8QH

*Central Services Unit*
Armstrong House
Oxford Road
Manchester M1 7ED
(for current and forward vacancies and AGCAS information booklets)

*Educational Counselling and Credit Transfer Information Services*
Fulton House
Jessop Avenue
Cheltenham GL50 3SH

*Equal Opportunities Commission*
Overseas House
Quay Street
Manchester M3 3HN

*European Women's Management Development Network*
c/o Domino Training Limited
56 Charnwood Road
Shepsted
Leicestershire LE12 9NP

*Industry Matters*
Royal Society of Arts
8 John Adam Street
London WC2N 6EZ

*National Association of Educational Guidance Service*
c/o Education and Training Shop
11 Clarence Street
Wolverhampton WV1 4JL

*National Council for Civil Liberties*
Rights for Women Unit
21 Tabard Street
London SE1 4LA

*National Extension College*
18 Brooklands Avenue
Cambridge CB2 2HN

*National Institute of Adult Education*
196 de Montfort Street
Leicester LE1 7GE

*National Organisation for Women's Management Education*
c/o Pepperell Unit
Industrial Society
Robert Hyde House
48 Bryanston Square
London W1H 7LN

*National Union of Students*
461 Holloway Road
London N7 6LJ

*New Ways to Work*
309 Upper Street
London N1 2TY

*Open College*
101 Wigmore Street
London W1H 9AA

*Open University*
Walton Hall
Milton Keynes MK7 6AA

*Training Access Points* (TAP)
St Mary's House
Moorfoot
Sheffield S1 4PQ

*Training Agency*
St Mary's House
Moorfoot
Sheffield S1 4PQ

*University of the Third Age*
6 Parkside Gardens
London SW19 5EY

*Women in Enterprise*
St Gabriel's House
24 Laburnum Street
Wakefield WF1 3QS

*Women into Industry*
P O Box 320
Brightlingsea
Colchester CO7 0DX

*Women into Information Technology*
c/o IT Strategy Services
21 Eastbourne Avenue
London W3 6JN

*Women in Management*
64 Marryat Road
London SW19 5BN

*Women Returners' Network*
c/o Ruth Michaels
100 Park Village East
London NW1 3SR

*Women and Training Group*
Hewmar House
120 London Road
Gloucester GL1 3PL

*Workers' Educational Association*
9 Upper Berkeley Street
London W1H 8BY

## Disabled jobhunters

Special help is available for disabled jobhunters. Local offices of the Training Agency Employment Service can offer assistance and copies of the *Code of Good Practice on the Employment of Disabled People* are available from them. The new TECs will also have a role to play. In addition to the various agencies linked with specific disabilities, advice is available from:

> *Disabled Graduates Careers Information Service*
> c/o University of Reading
> Careers Advisory Service
> Bulmershe Court
> Woodlands Avenue
> Earley
> Reading RG6 1HY
>
> *Disabled Living Foundation*
> 380–384 Harrow Road
> London W9 2HU

### Further reading

Thompson, M (1986), *Employment for Disabled People*, London, Kogan Page.

## Overseas students

As relatively few overseas students either want or are able to stay on after the completion of their studies, no special reference is included in the text. However, individual careers services often carry details of vacancies for nationals of specific countries and hold information about the procedures for obtaining work permits etc. It is impossible to generalise about the arrangements made by individual countries to aid students' return.

More information is available from:

> *Home Office, Immigration and Nationality Department*
> Lunar House
> Wellesley Road
> Croydon CR9 2BY
>
> *United Kingdom Council for Overseas Student Affairs*
> 60 Westbourne Grove
> London W2 5FG

*World University Service*
20–21 Compton Terrace
London N1 2UN

For an assessment of the experience of women overseas students in the UK, see Goldsmith, J and Shawcross, V (1985), *It Ain't Half Sexist, Mum*, London, UKCOSA and WUS.

Any complaints about cases of racial discrimination can be addressed in the first instance to:

*Commission for Racial Equality*
10–12 Allington Street
London SW1E 5EH

*Appendix 1*

# Background Statistics

For readers who like to put their own circumstances in a broader context, the following selection of statistics may prove illuminating. Note that there is usually a considerable time lag in the production of official statistics.

The following figures about the labour force, working patterns and educational attainment in Great Britain are compilations from official sources for *The Fact About Women Is . . .* (1989) published by the Equal Opportunities Commission and reproduced with permission.

| POPULATION | **1987** | |
|---|---|---|
| | Millions | |
| TOTAL POPULATION: GREAT BRITAIN | 56.9 | |

| Expressed as a percentage of the total population those aged: | 1987 | |
|---|---|---|
| | *Females* % | *Males* % |
| under 15 | 9.1 | 9.7 |
| 15 to state pension age | 29.9 | 32.9 |
| over state pension age | 12.1 | 6.1 |
| All ages | 51.1 | 48.7 |

(*Source:* OPCS)

ADULT POPULATION BY SEX AND MARITAL STATUS: GREAT BRITAIN

| All aged 16 and over | 1987 | |
|---|---|---|
| | *Females* % | *Males* % |
| Single | 22 | 30 |
| Married (includes separated) | 58 | 62 |
| Widowed | 14 | 4 |
| Divorced | 6 | 5 |

(*Source:* CSO Social Trends 1988)

117

FAMILIES BY TYPE: GREAT BRITAIN

|  |  | 1986<br>% |
|---|---|---|
| Married couple |  | 86 |
| Lone mother |  | 13 |
| of which: | Single | 3 |
|  | Widowed | 1 |
|  | Divorced | 6 |
|  | Separated | 3 |
| Lone father |  | 1 |
| All lone parents |  | 14 |

(*Source:* General Household Survey, 1986)


## EMPLOYMENT

ALL IN EMPLOYMENT: GREAT BRITAIN

| | 1987 Thousands | | | |
|---|---|---|---|---|
| | *Females* | | *Males* | |
| | full-time | part-time | full-time | part-time |
| All | 5,274.9 | 4,968.6 | 12,818.1 | 1,035.6 |
| Agriculture, forestry and fishing | 54.2 | 62.0 | 387.6 | 35.2 |
| Energy and water supply | 64.3 | 16.0 | 487.1 | 2.8 |
| Extraction of minerals/<br> manufactured metals | 136.3 | 39.9 | 563.9 | 9.1 |
| Metal goods, engineering etc | 397.5 | 119.6 | 1,922.9 | 36.7 |
| Other manufacturing industries | 632.2 | 242.0 | 1,378.7 | 59.1 |
| Construction | 83.6 | 85.8 | 1,593.4 | 61.2 |
| Distribution, hotels and repairs | 1,068.3 | 1,590.1 | 2,018.5 | 270.6 |
| of which: Retail distribution | 655.3 | 961.1 | 987.8 | 163.5 |
| Hotels and catering | 235.8 | 512.1 | 267.2 | 68.3 |
| Transport and communications | 229.1 | 83.0 | 1,141.2 | 36.1 |
| Banking, finance etc | 795.1 | 349.9 | 1,161.8 | 80.8 |
| of which: Business services | 365.2 | 203.4 | 627.7 | 56.4 |
| Other services | 1,801.9 | 2,370.9 | 2,127.6 | 442.6 |
| Workplace outside UK | 3.3 | 0.7 | 15.6 | – |
| Inadequately described/not<br> available | 9.2 | 8.4 | 19.9 | 1.4 |

(*Source:* Department of Employment)

EMPLOYMENT BY OCCUPATION: GREAT BRITAIN

| Occupational group | Men | | Women | |
|---|---|---|---|---|
| | 1987 | | | |
| | *Men* | | *Women* | |
| | Thousands | % | Thousands | % |
| I Professional and related supporting management and administration | 1,080 | 8 | 348 | 3 |
| II Professional and related in education, welfare and health | 724 | 5 | 1,465 | 14 |
| III Literary, artistic, sports | 186 | 1 | 126 | 1 |
| IV Professional and related in science, engineering, technology and similar fields | 966 | 7 | 107 | 1 |
| V Management | 1,763 | 13 | 638 | 6 |
| VI Clerical and related | 945 | 7 | 3,129 | 30 |
| VII Selling | 654 | 5 | 1,012 | 10 |
| VIII Security and protective services | 379 | 3 | 40 | 0 |
| IX Catering, cleaning, hairdressing and other personal services | 545 | 4 | 2,279 | 22 |
| X Farming, fishing and related | 353 | 3 | 82 | 1 |
| XI Processing, making, repairing and related (excluding metal and electrical) | 1,124 | 8 | 469 | 5 |
| XII Processing, making, repairing and related (metal and electrical) | 2,234 | 16 | 105 | 1 |
| XIII Painting, repetitive assembling, product inspection, packing and related | 505 | 4 | 360 | 3 |
| XIV Construction and mining | 834 | 6 | 10 | 0 |
| XV Transport operating, materials moving and storing | 1,393 | 10 | 77 | 1 |
| XVI Miscellaneous | 198 | 1 | 20 | 0 |
| Inadequately described not stated | 30 | 0 | – | – |
| All persons in employment | 13,951 | 100 | 10,296 | 100 |

(*Source:* Labour Force Survey, 1987)

**THE LABOUR FORCE 1987**

ECONOMICALLY ACTIVE PEOPLE

| Age | Men economically active | Thousands activity rate | Unemployment rate |
|---|---|---|---|
| | Thousands | % | % |
| 16–19 | 1,244 | 73 | 20 |
| 20–24 | 2,084 | 91 | 15 |
| 25–34 | 3,822 | 96 | 11 |
| 35–49 | 5,050 | 95 | 8 |
| 50–59 | 2,445 | 85 | 10 |
| 60–64 | 760 | 55 | 11 |
| 65+ | 262 | 8 | 8 |

| Age | Married women economically active | Activity rate | Unemployment rate |
|---|---|---|---|
| | Thousands | % | % |
| 16–19 | 50 | 55 | 26 |
| 20–24 | 647 | 63 | 16 |
| 25–34 | 1,968 | 63 | 13 |
| 35–49 | 3,317 | 73 | 6 |
| 50–59 | 1,396 | 60 | 5 |
| 60–64 | 206 | 20 | 5 |
| 65+ | 64 | 3 | – |

| Age | Non-married women economically active | Activity rate | Unemployment rate |
|---|---|---|---|
| | Thousands | % | % |
| 16–19 | 1,125 | 72 | 16 |
| 20–24 | 978 | 80 | 12 |
| 25–34 | 595 | 76 | 12 |
| 35–49 | 575 | 76 | 13 |
| 50–59 | 381 | 62 | 13 |
| 60–64 | 82 | 17 | – |
| 65+ | 72 | 15 | – |

(*Source:* Labour Force Survey, 1987)

## ALL IN EMPLOYMENT, INCLUDING SELF-EMPLOYED: GREAT BRITAIN

1987

Thousands

|  | Married | % | Non-married | % | Married | % |
|---|---|---|---|---|---|---|
|  | *Females* | | | | *Males* | |
| – full-time | 3,170 | 46 | 2,361 | 75 | 12,980 | 95 |
| – part-time | 3,785 | 54 | 794 | 25 | 646 | 5 |
|  | 6,961 | 100 | 3,159 | 100 | 13,638 | 100 |

(*Source:* Labour Force Survey, 1987)

## UNEMPLOYMENT: GREAT BRITAIN

January 1989
Thousands

|  | *Females* | *Males* |
|---|---|---|
| Registered unemployed | 571.8 | 1,391.4 |
| Unemployment rate | 4.9% | 8.6% |

(*Source:* Department of Employment Gazette)

**WOMEN ONLY**

WORKING STATUS OF WOMEN AGED 16–59: GREAT BRITAIN

Women aged 16–59 by marital status

| The % of women who | 1986 | | |
|---|---|---|---|
| | Work full-time | Work part-time | All economically active |
| Single | 56 | 14 | 80 |
| Widowed, divorced or separated | 31 | 23 | 61 |
| All non-married | 49 | 16 | 75 |
| Married | 28 | 33 | 66 |
| All women | 35 | 28 | 69 |

(*Source:* General Household Survey, 1986)

WORKING MOTHERS: GREAT BRITAIN

Mothers aged 16–59 by age of youngest child

| The % of mothers whose youngest child is: | 1986 | | |
|---|---|---|---|
| | Work full-time | Work part-time | All economically active |
| 0–2 years | 8 | 19 | 34 |
| 3–4 years | 12 | 33 | 50 |
| 5–9 years | 14 | 46 | 65 |
| 10 years and over | 28 | 42 | 73 |
| All with dependent children | 17 | 36 | 58 |
| All without dependent children | 48 | 22 | 77 |

(*Source:* General Household Survey, 1986)

TRENDS OVER TIME

EARNINGS: GREAT BRITAIN

Average gross hourly earnings, excluding the effects of over-time, full-time employees on adult rates

| | 1971 pence per hour | 1981 pence per hour | 1987 pence per hour |
|---|---|---|---|
| Women | 47.2 | 241.2 | 386.2 |
| Men | 74.1 | 331.2 | 526.2 |
| Differential | 26.9 | 90.0 | 140.0 |
| Women's earnings as a % of men's | 63.7 | 72.8 | 73.4 |

(*Source:* Department of Employment Gazette)

**EDUCATION**

SCHOOL EXAMINATIONS: ENGLAND AND WALES

1986–1987

Thousands

| Attempted CSE/O Level in: | *Girls* | *Boys* |
|---|---|---|
| English language | 328.9 | 321.9 |
| Maths | 307.2 | 309.8 |
| Biology | 199.0 | 110.2 |
| French | 152.6 | 99.2 |
| History | 133.9 | 132.6 |
| Chemistry | 93.5 | 121.4 |
| Physics | 74.1 | 189.8 |
| Computer science | 76.0 | 222.1 |

| GCE A Level | Attempts | Passes | Attempts | Passes |
|---|---|---|---|---|
| English | 29.7 | 24.4 | 12.9 | 10.5 |
| Maths | 18.3 | 13.8 | 37.8 | 28.5 |
| Physics | 7.9 | 6.0 | 28.1 | 21.9 |
| Other science subjects | 2.1 | 1.6 | 6.9 | 5.6 |

(*Source:* Statistics of School Leavers CSE and GCE, England, 1987.
DES. Summer examination results, 1987. Welsh Joint
Education Committee)

DESTINATION OF SCHOOL LEAVERS: ENGLAND AND WALES

1986–1987

Thousands

| | *Girls* | *Boys* |
|---|---|---|
| Degree courses | 24.8 | 32.1 |
| Teacher training courses | 1.7 | 0.4 |
| Other full-time further and higher education courses | 97.6 | 63.3 |
| Pupils leaving for employment/unemployment and destination not known | 243.6 | 283.6 |
| All leavers | 372.2 | 387.7 |

(*Source:* Statistics of School Leavers CSE and GCE, England, 1987.
DES. Statistics of Education in Wales. 1987 Welsh Office)

FULL-TIME UNDERGRADUATES AT BRITISH UNIVERSITIES
(UK DOMICILED)

| Degree subject | 1986–1987 | |
| --- | --- | --- |
| | Thousands | |
| | *Females* | *Males* |
| Languages and related | 18.3 | 7.7 |
| Social sciences | 14.8 | 17.1 |
| Multi-disciplinary studies | 12.7 | 15.0 |
| Medicine and dentistry | 9.9 | 12.0 |
| Biological sciences | 8.5 | 7.2 |
| Humanities | 6.7 | 7.5 |
| Physical sciences | 4.9 | 14.7 |
| Studies allied to medicine | 4.2 | 1.9 |
| Mathematical sciences | 3.4 | 10.1 |
| Business and financial studies | 3.4 | 5.2 |
| Engineering and technology | 2.7 | 24.3 |
| Veterinary science, agriculture and related | 2.1 | 2.4 |
| Creative arts | 2.1 | 1.4 |
| Education | 1.7 | 0.5 |
| Architecture and related | 0.8 | 2.2 |
| Librarianship and information science | 0.1 | 0.1 |
| All subjects | 96.3 | 129.3 |

(*Source:* DES University Statistics Volume 1 Students and Staff
1986–87)

**EUROPEAN FEMALE EMPLOYMENT**

CIVILIAN WORKING POPULATION (EXCLUDING ARMED FORCES)
EXPRESSED AS A PERCENTAGE OF FEMALES IN TOTAL WORKING POPULATION

| | EC.12 % | Belgium % | Denmark % | Holland % | Greece % | Spain % | France % | Ireland % | Italy % | Luxemburg % | Holland % | Portugal % | United Kingdom % |
|---|---|---|---|---|---|---|---|---|---|---|---|---|---|
| 1978 | 36.4 | 37.0 | 43.6 | 38.3 | 30.4 | 29.1 | 39.9 | 27.7 | 32.9 | 32.2 | 29.9 | 39.7 | 38.9 |
| 1980 | 37.1 | 38.1 | 44.6 | 38.6 | 30.0 | 29.3 | 40.8 | 28.2 | 34.0 | 32.5 | 32.0 | 41.2 | 39.6 |
| 1982 | 37.6 | 39.1 | 45.1 | 39.0 | 31.4 | 29.8 | 41.5 | 29.3 | 34.6 | 34.0 | 33.8 | 42.3 | 39.5 |
| 1984 | 38.4 | 40.0 | 45.6 | 39.3 | 34.6 | 30.4 | 42.3 | 29.8 | 35.5 | 35.4 | 34.8 | 41.6 | 40.5 |
| 1986 | 39.0 | 41.1 | 46.1 | 39.7 | 35.6 | 31.2 | 43.0 | 30.1 | 36.5 | 36.0 | 35.4 | 39.5 | 41.3 |

*Source:* Eurcstat Employment and Unemployment, 1988)

(Extract from *The Fact About Women Is...* (1989). Equal Opportunities Commission.)

# STUDENTS IN HIGHER EDUCATION

SOME RELEVANT STATISTICS FROM SOCIAL TRENDS 20, CENTRAL STATISTICAL OFFICE, HMSO, 1990

HIGHER EDUCATION – FULL-TIME STUDENTS: BY ORIGIN, SEX AND AGE

Thousands and percentages

| | Males | | | | | Females | | | | |
|---|---|---|---|---|---|---|---|---|---|---|
| | 1970 /71 | 1975 /76 | 1980 /81 | 1985 /86 | 1987 /88 | 1970 /71 | 1975 /76 | 1980 /81 | 1985 /86 | 1987 /88 |
| **Full-time students by origin** | | | | | | | | | | |
| From the United Kingdom | | | | | | | | | | |
| Universities[1] – post-graduate | 23.9 | 23.2 | 20.7 | 21.0 | 20.6 | 8.0 | 10.2 | 11.3 | 12.6 | 13.3 |
| – first degree | 128.3 | 130.1 | 145.1 | 134.3 | 135.4 | 57.0 | 73.6 | 96.2 | 99.9 | 103.5 |
| – other[2] | | | | 1.5 | 1.1 | | | | 1.2 | 1.2 |
| Polytechnics and colleges | 102.0 | 109.3 | 111.9 | 143.5 | 147.3[4] | 113.1 | 120.1 | 96.4 | 132.2 | 142.8[4] |
| Total full-time UK students | 254.2 | 262.6 | 277.7 | 300.4 | 304.4 | 178.2 | 203.8 | 203.9 | 245.9 | 260.9 |
| From abroad | 20.0 | 38.6 | 40.7 | 38.4 | 41.6 | 4.4 | 9.9 | 12.6 | 15.3 | 19.9 |
| Total full-time students | 274.2 | 301.2 | 318.4 | 338.7 | 346.1 | 182.6 | 213.7 | 216.5 | 261.3 | 280.8 |
| **Full-time students by age** *(percentages)* | | | | | | | | | | |
| 18 years and under | 10 | 11[3] | 16 | 15 | 15 | 17 | 14[3] | 19 | 17 | 17 |
| 19–20 years | 36 | 35 | 37 | 38 | 37 | 45 | 42 | 41 | 42 | 40 |
| 21–24 years | 38 | 36 | 30 | 29 | 31 | 24 | 28 | 25 | 26 | 28 |
| 25 years and over | 15 | 19 | 17 | 18 | 17 | 14 | 16 | 15 | 15 | 16 |

1. Origin is on fee-paying status except for EC students domiciled outside the United Kingdom who from 1980–81 are charged home rates but are included with students from abroad. From 1984 origin is based on students' usual places of domicile.
2. University first diplomas and certificates
3. In 1980 measurement by age changed from 31 December to 31 August.
4. Data for Northern Ireland relate to 1986–87.

(*Source:* Education Statistics for the United Kingdom, Department of Education and Science)

The number of students on full-time higher education courses in the United Kingdom rose by 17 per cent between 1980–81 and 1987–88 to stand at 627,000. This increase has been entirely confined to polytechnics and colleges, with university numbers remaining almost constant. Over two-thirds of the increase can be attributed to the increase in the number of female students. In 1987–88, 55 per cent of full-time, higher education United Kingdom students were male compared to 60 per cent in 1980–81. The number of students from abroad increased by two and one half times between 1970–71 and 1987–88.

Between 1970–71 and 1987–88 the number of students in part-time higher education in the United Kingdom more than doubled to stand at 367,000. The Open University accounted for 12 per cent of part-time students when it opened in 1970–71, but by 1987–88 this proportion had risen to 23 per cent. The increase in part-time higher education has taken place almost entirely among those aged over 25 years. Women accounted for 39 per cent of part-time students in 1987–88 compared to only 14 per cent in 1970–71. Overall, women accounted for 43 per cent of students in full-time and part-time higher education in 1987–88 compared to only 33 per cent in 1970–71.

HIGHER EDUCATION – PART-TIME STUDENTS:[1] BY TYPE OF ESTABLISHMENT, SEX AND AGE

Thousands and percentages

| | Males | | | | | Females | | | | |
|---|---|---|---|---|---|---|---|---|---|---|
| | 1970 /71 | 1975 /76 | 1980 /81 | 1985 /86 | 1987 /88 | 1970 /71 | 1975 /76 | 1980 /81 | 1985 /86 | 1987 /88 |
| **Part-time students by establishment** | | | | | | | | | | |
| Universities | 18.1 | 19.3 | 22.6 | 26.3 | 27.6 | 5.7 | 7.0 | 10.7 | 16.0 | 18.5 |
| Open University[2] | 14.3 | 33.6 | 37.6 | 41.7 | 45.4 | 5.3 | 22.0 | 30.1 | 36.0 | 40.4 |
| Polytechnics and colleges | | | | | | | | | | |
| – part-time day courses | 69.8 | 80.2 | 110.5 | 112.2 | 115.1[3] | 6.7 | 15.4 | 30.8 | 49.9 | 61.2[3] |
| – evening only courses | 39.8 | 35.0 | 35.1 | 34.4 | 36.0[3] | 5.0 | 5.8 | 15.2 | 20.3 | 22.4[3] |
| Total part-time students | 142.0 | 168.1 | 205.7 | 214.6 | 224.1 | 22.7 | 50.2 | 86.8 | 122.2 | 142.5 |
| **Part-time students by age** *(percentages)* | | | | | | | | | | |
| 18 years and under | .. | .. | 6 | 4 | 4 | | | 4 | 2 | 2 |
| 19–20 | .. | .. | 16 | 14 | 13 | | | 9 | 7 | 7 |
| 21–24 | .. | .. | 23 | 22 | 21 | | | 18 | 17 | 17 |
| 25 and over | .. | .. | 54 | 60 | 63 | | | 69 | 73 | 74 |

1. Excludes students enrolled on nursing and paramedical courses at Department of Health establishments; some 94,000 in 1987–88.
2. Calendar years beginning in second year shown. Excludes short course students up to 1982–83. In 1986–87 and 1987–88 there were respectively 8,400 and 10,400 specialised course students for whom data by sex were not available; these have been excluded.
3. Data for Northern Ireland to 1986–87.

(*Source:* Education Statistics for the United Kingdom, Department of Education and Science)

# Access for women

In 1990 the Universities Information Unit, Committee of Vice Chancellors and Principals produced a University factsheet which included a supplement on women. This document graphically highlights the fact that throughout the 1960s the percentage of female applicants to university remained more or less constant at about 30 per cent. This rose through the 1970s, reached 40 per cent in 1980 and by 1988 stood at about 46 per cent, with 48.8 per cent of acceptances being of women. All the signs are that this upward trend will continue. This change reflects the larger number of women students now staying on to post-compulsory education in school as well as an increasing number of mature applicants.

There is a marked difference in subject preference between women and men, but over an 18-year period from 1968 to 1986, women increased their presence in all subjects, though they still make up only 10 per cent of applicants for engineering, for example. More than half the students entering medicine and allied subjects are now women.

PROPORTION OF WOMEN IN SOME TOP (AND OTHER GOOD) JOBS, 1986

| | | |
|---|---|---|
| Bank managers | Under 2% | |
| Members of Institute of Directors | 2·9% | |
| British Institute of Management members | 3·4% | |
| Institute of Chartered Accountants full members | 7% | (student members: 32%) |
| Chartered Institute of Management Accountants full members | 3·5% | (student members: 20%) |
| Institution of Civil Engineers full members | below 1% | (students: 8%) |
| Institution of Electrical Engineers full members | below 1% | (student members: about 5·8%) |
| Institution of Mechanical Engineers full members | below 1% | (student members: about 4%) |
| Engineering technicians | 3% | (trainees: 5%) |
| Ophthalmic opticians | 27% | (students: 56%) |
| Dentists – practising | 20% | (dental students: about 44%) |
| Medicine: general practitioners (principals) | 19% | (entrants to medical school, 1986: 46%) |
| General surgeons – consultants | 1% | (registrars: 5%) |

| | | |
|---|---|---|
| Gynaecologists/obstetricians – consultants | 30% | (registrars: 30%) |
| Paediatricians – consultants | 19% | (registrars: 37%) |
| Barristers – practising | 13% | (students: 38%) |
| Solicitors – with practice certificates | 15% | (students: 48%) |
| Royal Institution of Chartered Surveyors full members | well below 2% | (student members: 9%) |
| Society of Surveying Technicians | well below 1% | |
| Architects – practising | 7% | (students: 25%) |
| Veterinary surgeons | 16% | (students: about 47%) |
| Advertising account executives | 26% | |
| Air traffic control officers | 6% | (trainees: 16%) |
| Driving examiners | 6% | |
| Local authority chief executives | well below 1% | |
| Town planners | 20% | |
| Principals of further education colleges | 6% | |
| Lecturers/assistants in higher education | 13% | |
| Professors | 3% | |
| Civil Service: | | |
| Executive Officers (fairly junior grade) | 44% | |
| Principals and above | 7% | |
| Administration Trainees (high-flyer graduate entrants) | 27% | |

(Reproduced with permission from *Equal Opportunities: A Careers Guide for Women and Men* (1987) Anna Alston and Ruth Miller, Penguin.)

## TRENDS IN TWO DIFFERENT OCCUPATIONAL AREAS (CHARTERED ACCOUNTANCY AND PHARMACY)

The entry of increasing numbers of women into professional areas has widespread implications, illustrated in the following extracts from *Gendered Jobs and Social Change* (1990) Rosemary Crompton and Kay Sanderson, Unwin Hyman. Reproduced with permission.

ICAEW MEMBERS, 1986: EMPLOYMENT, LOCATION AND AGE, HOME MEMBERS ONLY (PERCENTAGES BY ROW)

| Age: | Partner in practice/ sole practice | | Employed in a practice | | Commerce or industry | | Other | | Total numbers | |
|---|---|---|---|---|---|---|---|---|---|---|
| | M | F | M | F | M | F | M | F | M | F |
| Under 36 | 15 | 8 | 36 | 44 | 37 | 20 | 13 | 28 | 20,555 | 4,482 |
| 36–45 | 36 | 31 | 8 | 22 | 50 | 28 | 5 | 19 | 20,443 | 793 |
| 46–55 | 38 | 41 | 4 | 18 | 52 | 30 | 6 | 11 | 11,558 | 157 |
| 55+ | 45 | 44 | 7 | 13 | 40 | 19 | 8 | 24 | 6,899 | 62 |

### 1987 FIGURES

| Age: | M | F | M | F | M | F | M | F | M | F |
|---|---|---|---|---|---|---|---|---|---|---|
| 23–26 | (0.4) | (0.3) | 39 | 41 | 8 | 6 | 52 | 53 | 1,612 | 623 |
| 27–31 | 7 | 5 | 45 | 50 | 32 | 25 | 12 | 20 | 9,888 | 2,651 |
| 32–36 | 26 | 18 | 23 | 32 | 47 | 28 | 4 | 22 | 10,487 | 1,617 |
| 37+ | 39 | 34 | 6 | 21 | 49 | 27 | 5 | 18 | 37,994 | 1,011 |

(*Source:* ICAEW membership statistics. These are collected via a retention form attached to the subscription and the response rate is 94 per cent. Details relating to partnerships/employment in public practice and commerce or industry are likely to be accurate. The 'other' category includes (a) those not responding to the questionnaire (6 per cent), (b) those not in permanent employment and (c) those recently admitted to membership who have not yet been sent a questionnaire, as well as those in other employment such as teaching. The distribution of ICAEW members between the latter three categories is not known, and will clearly have a substantial impact on the percentages in the younger age ranges.)

*Continued on page* 134.

FIRST DESTINATIONS OF GRADUATES (SIX MONTHS AFTER GRADUATION)

# 1 All subjects – men and women

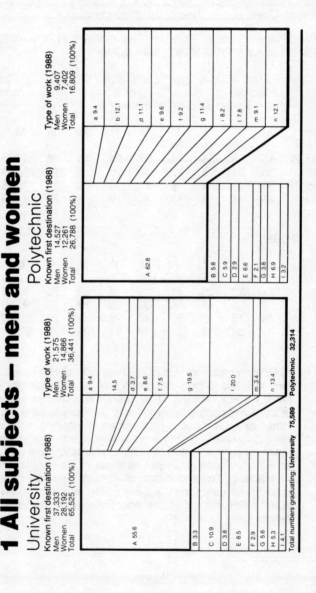

## University

**Known first destination (1988)**
Men 37,333
Women 28,192
Total 65,525 (100%)

**Type of work (1988)**
Men 21,575
Women 14,866
Total 36,441 (100%)

A 55.6
B 3.3
C 10.9
D 3.8
E 8.5
F 2.9
G 5.6
H 5.3
I 4.1

a 9.4
14.5
d 3.7
e 8.6
f 7.5
g 19.5
l 20.0
m 3.4
n 13.4

## Polytechnic

**Known first destination (1988)**
Men 14,527
Women 12,261
Total 26,788 (100%)

**Type of work (1988)**
Men 9,407
Women 7,402
Total 16,809 (100%)

A 62.8
B 5.8
C 5.9
D 2.9
E 6.6
F 2.1
G 3.8
H 6.9
I 3.2

a 9.4
b 12.1
d 11.1
e 9.6
f 9.2
g 11.4
i 8.2
l 7.8
m 9.1
n 12.1

Total numbers graduating: University **75,589** Polytechnic **32,314**

*What Do Graduates Do?* (1990) Association of Graduate Careers Advisory Services, Hobsons Publishing. Reproduced with permission.

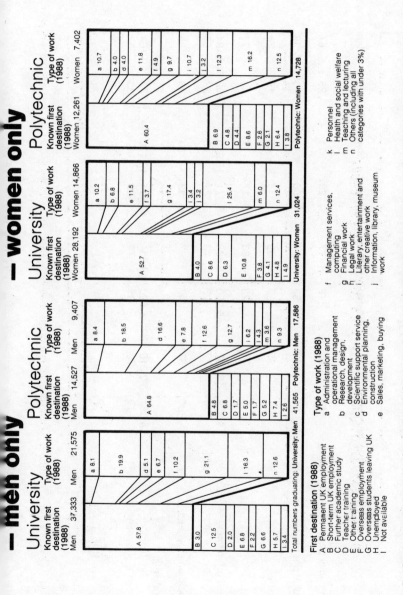

*What Do Graduates Do?* (1990) Association of Graduate Careers Advisory Services, Hobsons Publishing. Reproduced with permission.

MEN AND WOMEN IN PHARMACY: SELECTED YEARS, BY OCCUPATION

| | 1963 % | | 1972 % | | 1977 % | | 1981 % | | 1985 % | |
|---|---|---|---|---|---|---|---|---|---|---|
| | Men | Women | Men | Women | Men | Women | Men | Women | Men | Women |
| (1) Community pharmacy | 84 | 16 | 82 | 18 | 77 | 23 | 71 | 29 | 67 | 33 |
| (2) Hospital pharmacy | 45 | 55 | 37 | 63 | 44 | 56 | 40 | 60 | 38 | 62 |
| (3) Industry | 95 | 5 | 95 | 5 | 89 | 11 | 85 | 15 | 78 | 22 |
| (4) Other | 82 | 18 | 77 | 23 | 83 | 17 | 77 | 23 | 76 | 24 |
| (5) Total (a) Number | 20,284 | 4,378 | 18,400 | 5,380 | 16,498 | 5,971 | 16,315 | 7,809 | 16,194 | 9,455 |
| (b) Per cent | 82 | 18 | 77 | 23 | 73 | 27 | 68 | 32 | 63 | 37 |
| (6) No paid employment | 70 | 30 | 53 | 47 | 67 | 33 | 64 | 36 | 65 | 35 |
| (7) Overall total (a) Number | 21,401 | 4,861 | 20,010 | 6,800 | 19,604 | 7,504 | 19,130 | 9,373 | 19,164 | 11,089 |
| (b) Per cent | 81 | 19 | 75 | 25 | 72 | 28 | 67 | 33 | 67 | 37 |

*Notes:*

Data derived from the *Pharmaceutical Journal*, vols. 193, p. 124; 209, p. 228; 219, p. 462; 228, p. 131; March 1986, p. 265. Data for 1963 and 1972 were collected via a sample survey of members, for 1977 onwards, as part of a retention from an application form completed by all members. The apparent fluctuations in row 6 (no paid employment) are a consequence both of changes in classification and rules relating to the subscriptions of non-working but registered pharmacists. Row 5 and above, therefore, represent the most accurate estimates of gender distribution.

However, it is also apparent that some pharmacists recording no occupation *do* work part time (see, for example, *Pharmaceutical Journal*, 1972, p. 230, Table 6), although the numbers are small and do not affect major trends. The figures in this table, therefore, should be regarded as fairly accurate estimates, rather than as giving precise numbers.

## AGE PROFILE OF GRADUATES

UNIVERSITIES, POLYTECHNICS AND COLLEGES – ALL SUBJECTS – 1987 EXCLUDING OVERSEAS STUDENTS RETURNING HOME

| | Total under 25 | | 25–29 | | 30–34 | | 35–39 | | 40–49 | |
|---|---|---|---|---|---|---|---|---|---|---|
| | U | P/C | U | P/C | U | P/C | U | P/C | U | P/C |
| A | 58.9 | 64.7 | 67.4 | 62.1 | 49.2 | 56.8 | 46.0 | 59.8 | 45.8 | 61.5 |
| B | 3.3 | 6.0 | 2.1 | 5.7 | 3.7 | 4.7 | 2.1 | 5.1 | 3.5 | 5.6 |
| C | 11.4 | 4.8 | 10.7 | 7.2 | 16.8 | 8.9 | 15.3 | 6.9 | 13.7 | 4.8 |
| D | 4.7 | 4.5 | 2.8 | 3.5 | 7.5 | 5.7 | 8.5 | 9.7 | 9.5 | 5.2 |
| E | 9.0 | 6.2 | 7.6 | 6.2 | 9.9 | 7.1 | 11.9 | 6.1 | 9.5 | 5.0 |
| F | 3.1 | 2.5 | 2.1 | 2.0 | 2.4 | 0.5 | 1.5 | 0.5 | 0.9 | 0.2 |
| H | 6.1 | 8.9 | 5.4 | 10.4 | 7.7 | 12.7 | 9.4 | 8.7 | 9.5 | 13.7 |
| I | 3.4 | 2.4 | 2.0 | 2.9 | 2.8 | 3.6 | 5.3 | 3.2 | 7.4 | 3.8 |
| Total | 51,798 | 30,434 | 3,131 | 2,169 | 907 | 995 | 907 | 724 | 430 | 496 |

*Key:*  A  Permanent UK employment  C  Further academic study  E  Other training  H  Believed unemployed
B  Short-term employment  D  Teacher training  F  Overseas employment  (31 December)
U  Universities  I  Not available
P/C  Polytechnics and Colleges

(Reproduced with permission from *What Do Graduates Do?* (1990) Association of Graduate Careers Advisory Services, Hobsons

## Appendix 2
# Discrimination and the Law

The following extracts from the 1975 Sex Discrimination Act and from subsequent guidelines issued through the Home Office and the Equal Opportunities Commission elaborate some of the statements made elsewhere in this book about discrimination. Note the irony that, as with other legal documents, the Act itself refers only to 'he'.

'Discrimination'

The SDA deals with two sorts of discrimination, known as 'direct' and 'indirect'. With reference to employment, either sort can be on the ground of sex or on the ground of marriage. Thus there are four main categories to consider:

- Direct sex discrimination: which is to treat anyone, on the ground of his or her sex, less favourably than a person of the opposite sex is or would be treated in the same circumstances. Example: 'Male graduate required, with honours degree in chemistry, for teaching post beginning September.'

- Indirect sex discrimination: which arises where a requirement or condition, applied equally to men and women, has *in practice* a disproportionately adverse effect on people of one sex as compared with the other, and cannot be shown to be justified in terms of the job to be done, irrespective of sex. Example: 'Icecream seller (part-time) wanted; must be 6 ft tall.

- Direct marriage discrimination: which is to treat a married person, on the ground of his or her married status, less favourably than an unmarried person of the same sex is or would be treated. Example: 'Must be free to travel: no married applicants.'

- Indirect marriage discrimination: which arises where a requirement or condition, applied equally to married and unmarried people of the same sex, has *in practice* a disproportionately adverse effect on married as compared with unmarried people and cannot be shown to be justified in terms of the job to be done, irrespective of marital status. Example: 'This is a demanding job, unsuitable for applicants with family responsibilities'.

*NOTE: The important thing to remember in all this is that you can legiti-mately describe what a job involves, but that you cannot legitimately draw conclusions about the sex or marital status of applicants whom you would think suitable. Leave them to decide, according to what they know of their own circumstances, whether they could or could not cope with the job to be done.*

(Extract from *So You Think You've Got It Right. . .*
Equal Opportunities Commission (1983))

## Sex Discrimination Act, Section 38
### (Discriminatory Advertisements)

(1) It is unlawful to publish or cause to be published an advertisement which indicates, or might reasonably be understood as indicating, an intention by a person to do any act which is or might be unlawful by virtue of Part II or III.

(2) Subsection (1) does not apply to an advertisement if the intended act would not in fact be unlawful.

(3) For the purposes of subsection (1), use of a job description with a sexual connotation (such as 'waiter', 'salesgirl', 'postman' or 'stewardess') shall be taken to indicate an intention to discriminate, unless the advertisement contains an indication to the contrary.

(4) The publisher of an advertisement made unlawful by subsection (1) shall not be subject to any liability under that subsection in respect of the publication of the adverstisement if he proves:

(a) that the advertisement was published in reliance on a statement made to him by the person who caused it to be published to the effect that, by reason of the operation of subsection (2), the publication would not be lawful, and

(b) that it was reasonable for him to rely on the statement.

(5) A person who knowingly or recklessly makes a statement such as is referred to in subsection (4) which in a material respect is false or misleading commits an offence, and shall be liable on summary con-viction to a fine not exceeding £400.

(Extract from Sex Discrimination Act, 1975)

An individual who thinks that an advertisement is discriminatory would have to report it to the EOC, since only the Commission can enforce the rules on advertising. The EOC pamphlet 'EOC Advertis-ing Guidance' sets out guidelines for advertisers which should help employers to keep within the law. For example, it suggests that where jobs have been done traditionally by men, advertisements ought to state that applications from both sexes are invited.

## Interviews etc

The requirements not to discriminate apply to all the stages of selection.

In particular, the SDA provides that there should be no discrimination in the arrangements which are made for determining who should be offered a job.

This means that employers need to ensure that there is no discrimination in relation to:

(i)  job specifications, conditions or requirements;
(ii)  treatment of applicants;
(iii)  selection of applicants for interview;
(iv)  arrangements for interview.

An employer who refuses to interview female applicants is obviously directly discriminating; but since it may be difficult to prove a refusal if made on the telephone, it is always advisable to apply for a job in writing and to keep a copy of the letter. Even arrangements for interviews may discriminate against women. For example, unnecessarily long interviews involving one or two nights away from home might discourage female applicants with children.

More important perhaps is the interview itself. It is not unknown for employers still to react to a woman's wedding or engagement ring with a barrage of questions about her 'commitment to the job', whether or not she intends to have children etc. They would not dream of asking a man such questions. The EOC offers some helpful advice to employers:

> The requirement not to discriminate against married persons, or against women, can best be met by leaving questions relating to marital status and dependants to be followed up with the successful candidate after the appointment has been made. Similarly, when the applicant is being considered for a job previously done exclusively by members of the other sex, real difficulties of a practical kind may be envisaged by the interviewer. Any discussion of these difficulties should not be worded in such a way that they discourage the applicant.
>
> (*Guidance on Equal Opportunity Policies and Practices in Employment*)

## Selection of employees

A woman who is refused a job because of her sex will be able to claim discrimination whether or not someone else is offered the job. The employer will have to show that there were reasons other than her sex for refusing to offer her the job, or that the job is not covered by the SDA, or that being a man is a 'genuine occupational qualification' for the job.

(Extract from *Law at Work: Sex Discrimination*, Shelley Adams (1980), Sweet & Maxwell. Reproduced with permission)

## Genuine occupational qualification

s.7(1)     **3.11** Sex discrimination (but not discrimination against married persons or victimisation) by an employer in recruiting for a job, or in providing opportunities for promotion or transfer to, or training for, a job is not unlawful where a person's sex is a *genuine occupational qualification (GOQ)* for the job. The criteria for determining whether a person's sex is a *GOQ* for a particular job are set out in detail in the Act and are explained below. The *GOQ* is not an automatic exception for general categories of jobs: in every case it will be necessary for the employer to show, if the exception is to be claimed, that the criteria set out apply to the particular job in question.

**3.12** A person's sex is a *GOQ* for a job

s.7(2)*(a)*
(a) Where the essential nature of the job calls for a man (or woman) for reasons of physiology (excluding physical strength or stamina) – an example might be modelling clothes – or in dramatic performances or other entertainment for reasons of authenticity, so that in either case the essential nature of the job would be materially different if carried out by a person of the other sex.

s.7(2)*(b)*
(b) Where considerations of decency or privacy require the job to be held by a man (or woman), either because it is likely to involve physical contact between the jobholder and men (or women) in circumstances where they might reasonably object to the jobholder being of the opposite sex; or because the jobholder is likely to work in the presence of people who might reasonably object to the presence of a person of the opposite sex to themselves. It might be claimed, for example, that being a man was a *GOQ* by virtue of this provision for a job as a men's changing-room attendant.

s.7(2)*(c)*
(c) Where the nature or location of the establishment makes it impracticable for the jobholder to live in premises other than those provided by the employer (eg if the job is on a ship or on a remote site) and the only available premises for persons doing that kind of job do not provide both separate sleeping accommodation for each sex, and sanitary facilities which can be used by one sex in privacy from the other. In such a case, the employer may discriminate by choosing for the job only persons of the same sex as those who are already living, or who normally live, in those premises. However, the exception does not apply if the employer could reasonably be expected either to equip the premises with the necessary separate sleeping accommodation and separate or private sanitary facilities, or to provide other premises, for a jobholder of the opposite sex.

| | |
|---|---|
| s.7(2)(d) | (d) Where the job is in a single-sex establishment (eg a single-sex hospital), or in a single-sex part of an establishment, for persons requiring special care, supervision or attention and the essential character of that establishment, or the part of it within which the work is done, is such that it is reasonable to restrict the job to a person of the same sex as those for whom the establishment (or that part of it) exists. A single-sex institution which exceptionally admits persons of the other sex does not lose the right to claim the exception. However, the exception does not necessarily apply to all jobs in a single-sex establishment of the kind described: it will need to be shown in relation to any particular job that the character of the establishment requires *that job* to be held by a man (or woman). |
| s.7(2)(e) | (e) Where the holder of the job provides individuals with personal services promoting their welfare or education, or similar personal services, and those services can most effectively be provided by a man (or a woman). For example, some women might respond best to help offered by a female welfare worker. |
| s.7(2)(f) | (f) Where the job needs to be held by a man because of restrictions imposed by the laws regulating the employment of women. Factories legislation, for example, limits the times at which women may work in certain places. It may therefore be necessary for an employer to restrict to men certain jobs involving night work. |
| s.7(2)(g) | (g) Where the job involves work outside the United Kingdom in a country whose laws or customs are such that the job can only be done, or can only be done effectively, by a man (or woman). For example, a job might involve driving a car, but it is to be performed in a country where women are forbidden to drive. |
| s.7(2)(h) | (h) Where the job is one of two which are to be held by a married couple. |
| s.7(3),(4) | **3.13** In many cases, a job will not consist *entirely* of work which fulfils one of the *GOQ* criteria described above, but will contain some duties to which one of the criteria apply. For example, an assistant in a shop selling women's clothes may sometimes need to assist customers in the changing-room, and this might be a task to which the 'decency and privacy' *GOQ* (paragraph 3.12(b)) would apply. The *GOQ* exception will apply to the whole of such a job, unless the employer already has employees of the appropriate sex who are capable of carrying out the duties to which the *GOQ* would apply, whom it would be reasonable to employ on those duties, and whose numbers are sufficient to |

meet the employer's likely requirements without undue inconvenience. This will mean that, in the case of the clothes shop example, if there were a number of jobs for sales assistance, the *GOQ* could not necessarily be claimed successfully in respect of all of them on the grounds that any of them might need to undertake changing-room duties from time to time. It would only be lawful for the employer to ensure that he had enough female assistants to cover those changing-room duties which were likely to arise, after which the requirement not to discriminate would apply to access to the remaining jobs.

(Extract from *Guide to the Sex Discrimination Act, 1975*, HMSO)

## Sex Discrimination Act, Section 48
### (Other Discriminatory Training etc)

Section 48(1)

Nothing in Parts II to IV shall render unlawful any act done by an employer in relation to particular work in his employment, being an act done in, or in connection with,

  (a) affording his female employees only, or his male employees only, access to facilities for training which would help to fit them for that work, or

  (b) encouraging women only, or men only, to take advantage of opportunities for doing that work,

where at any time within the twelve months immediately preceding the doing of the act there were no persons of the sex in question among those doing that work or the number of persons of that sex doing the work was comparatively small.

(Extract from Sex Discrimination Act, 1975)

# Index